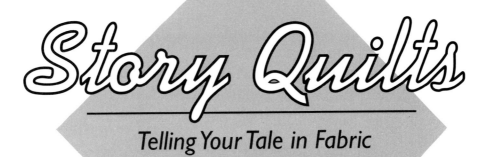

Story Quilts

Telling Your Tale in Fabric

MARY MASHUTA

C&T PUBLISHING

© Copyright 1992 by Mary Mashuta

Photographs by Sharon Risedorph, San Francisco, California, unless otherwise noted.

Editorial and art direction by Diane Pedersen, C&T Publishing.

Edited by Sayre Van Young, Berkeley, California.

Technical editing by Elizabeth Aneloski, C&T Publishing.

Design and production by Bobbi Sloan Design,
Berkeley, California.

Illustrations by Lisa Krieshok, Berkeley, California.

Published by C & T Publishing
P.O. Box 1456
Lafayette, CA 94549

ISBN: 0-914881-47-7

Mashuta, Mary.
    Story quilts: telling your tale in fabric / Mary Mashuta.
        p. cm.
    Includes bibliographical references (p.   ).
    ISBN 0-914881-47-7
        1. Patchwork. 2. Quilts—Themes, motives. I. Title.
TT835.M385 1992
746.9'7—dc20

Library of Congress Catalog Card Number: 91-58603
Printed in Hong Kong

Table of Contents

For my mother, Louise Adelaide Peterson Mashuta

(1912-1989)

*She let me sew from her scrapbag; she bought me
my first children's sewing machine; she let me
graduate to sewing on her Singer Featherweight
portable...she always thought what I made was
wonderful.*

Introduction

This book is about creative problem-solving, about learning how to create an image that tells a story in fabric. Story quilts don't all look like they've come from the same mold, as it is possible to use many different design formats when creating them. The common thread that unites them is that they are all narrative quilts—fabric, design, and color work together to tell a story.

In creating a story quilt, I use a specific experience as the starting place in my design process. Viewers may miss my story and concentrate on interpretations based on their own history. They may also prefer to scrutinize the size of my quilting stitches, whether my triangles have sharp points, or my color usage. This doesn't really matter; what's important to me is what I got out of the process of creation, and what I went through as I designed and stitched the piece. If someone likes the quilt, if it gets in a show or wins a ribbon, that's fine. However, that's not why I make story quilts. To me, the process of creation is far more important than the product.

Other than my own work, the quilts in this book were produced by students who have taken my story quilt class. For me, teaching the class has been an uplifting experience as quilters have opened up to share part of their personal history with me and their classmates. But since story quilts may be a new idea to you, it might be helpful if I answered some of the questions first-time story quilters often ask.

QUESTION: How much quilting skill do I need to make a story quilt?
ANSWER: I have worked with students at all levels beyond the very basic beginning level. You can start wherever you are in your development, but you may want to expand some of your skills if lack of expertise is keeping you from putting your concept into fabric.

QUESTION: How can I design my own story quilt? I've always used purchased patterns, copied quilts from books and magazines, or done class projects where we copied the teacher's project.
ANSWER: Being creative is just being able to find solutions. You do that every day. And when you discover the process involved in putting together a story quilt, step by step, you'll find it isn't so hard after all. The solution or end product becomes, simply speaking, your quilt. Many students have confessed that designing their story quilt was the first time they felt "creative" as far as quiltmaking was concerned. A large part of doing is knowing you "can" do.

QUESTION: How can I make my own story quilt if I can't find patterns for the blocks I want to use? I've never drafted my own patterns.
ANSWER: The basics of pattern drafting aren't hard once you understand that most blocks are based on some kind of grid. Knowing this enables you to draw most blocks. If a block is too difficult, find another that's simpler. Blocks don't have to be complicated to be meaningful. (Basic information about drafting appears in Chapter 9.)

QUESTION: I've only made traditional pieced block quilts. How can I step beyond this and make my own one-of-a-kind story quilt?
ANSWER: Traditional pieced blocks are a good starting point for a story quilt because they provide a "design backbone." Including them in your work is comforting because you're paying homage to past quiltmaking tradition. However, you can stretch and go beyond the narrative limitation that using pieced blocks alone can impose.

QUESTION: I've only made fast quilts because my time is limited and I want quick results. Is this going to keep me from making a story quilt?
ANSWER: You can still employ fast methods where they will work for the individual parts of your quilt. However, creating a story quilt offers all the opportunities of a more in-depth project. The creative process becomes enjoyable and important in and of itself. In creating a quilt that tells a personal story, you can take pleasure in the time spent thinking about the subject, as well as the time spent sewing.

QUESTION: How long will it take to make a story quilt?
ANSWER: Basically it takes as long as it takes. Some of my quilts from point of inspiration to completion took a few months, others took years. Yours will take as long as it needs to.

QUESTION: How big of a project should I plan for my first story quilt?

ANSWER: It's easy to get carried away and plan a quilt you will never have a hope of finishing in this lifetime. Begin by limiting the finished size; the physical dimensions will then become part of the input used to make decisions. Try starting with 36" x 36" or 45" x 54". Renegotiate with yourself later, if necessary.

QUESTION: I've never had anything spectacular happen to me. How can I make a story quilt?

ANSWER: Life happens minute-by-minute. It isn't necessary to have spectacular events to chronicle to make a meaningful story quilt. Begin by picking something simple.

QUESTION: I thought quilts were supposed to be beautiful. Some of the quilts in this book aren't about "pretty" topics.

ANSWER: When another quilter asked me the same question, I asked where she had read the rule that quilts were supposed to be beautiful. She got a funny look on her face when she realized the rule was just something she had made up in her own mind. Personal preferences aside, quilts don't have to be beautiful to be meaningful. Making a story quilt goes beyond making a beautiful quilt. It is the process of adding your soul to your work.

QUESTION: How can I come up with a color scheme that matches my subject? I'm unsure about color. I've always made quilts that matched the rooms in my house, copied other people's color schemes, or had the clerks at the quilt shop pick out my colors for me.

ANSWER: You can always consult a color wheel or a book on color for color scheme ideas, but don't lock yourself into a specific scheme too soon. The setting where your story occurred or specific emotions relating to your theme may suggest possible colors. Theme fabrics will also present possibilities. Keep an open mind and your color scheme will develop naturally.

Many of the story quilters tried a polychromatic color scheme (using all the colors on the color wheel). Others experimented with a subtle pushed-neutral color scheme. I discuss specific color usage for many of the quilts pictured here—perhaps that can provide a few ideas too!

QUESTION: How did the story quiltmakers find such interesting prints to help tell their stories? Very little "interesting" printed fabric is available where I live.

ANSWER: Part of the magic of finding the "perfect" story print is actually learning to be able to see it when you come upon it. For me, some of the pleasure in making story quilts comes from the process of looking for and collecting fabrics. The themes give a focus to my seemingly endless browsing in fabric shops!

QUESTION: Some of the quilts you included are very personal. I don't know about sharing myself with others, putting myself out there, so to speak.

ANSWER: Learn the process for making a story quilt by starting with a simple, noncharged subject like a happy childhood memory or a vacation. When the time comes to tackle a more difficult subject, you will know the process. Learn to make quilts for you first. You will discover it is wonderful when your work speaks to someone else, too.

QUESTION: All right, you convinced me. Where do I begin?

ANSWER: That's simple. Just sit back, put your feet up, and get comfortable. Since the quilts are probably what attracted you to this book to begin with, you'll want to get to them and their stories as soon as possible. You may be interested in specific designs or techniques as you read. Chapters 8 and 9 deal with this information. But first, let's go over the general process involved in creating a story quilt.

1. Creating a Story Quilt: The Process

The thought of beginning any quilt is often overwhelming. Where to begin? For story quilts, the answer is easy. Before design, before fabric, first find the story.

SELECTING A TOPIC

Since using your experiences as subject matter for a quilt may be a foreign concept for you, let's talk a moment about possible topics. Some of the people who take my workshops come with a specific topic in mind; others don't have a clue, but come just to learn the process involved. It's absolutely amazing the stories people have, even those who at first didn't think they had a story to share. And hearing the stories of others is often all that's needed to spark a memory and get the ball rolling. Perhaps reading about some of the quilts pictured in this book will have the same effect on you.

Begin with your own childhood or recall a story about a family member. What a perfect way to pass on family stories and traditions. Perhaps you would prefer something that has happened to you as an adult. Since many quilters work part- or full-time, maybe you have a job-related story to tell. And all of us have had to cope with the large and small disasters of life. You probably look forward to—and fondly back on—vacations. Why not remember a special trip by making a quilt about it? And lastly, you live in a particular historical time—why not make a social comment about what is happening to the world around you?

Once you have a general topic, you'll probably need to narrow your focus. For example, a student who wanted to work with a favorite trip she and her husband had taken brought a large box of pictures and his complete written journal to class. With so much material at hand, a sampler-type quilt seemed appropriate with individual pictures portraying memorable things they had seen. All of a sudden the task became monumental. How to fit it all into one quilt, what to select, what to leave out? This is the time to say "less is more."

At one time in my teaching career, I taught remedial English. Instead of asking my students to write on the familiar theme, "What I Did Last Summer," I asked them to select and describe only five minutes of their summer.

In the same way, you can limit your subject matter for a story quilt. Learning to select one or two images from a trip for a quilt will make your designing task far easier. The images still act as a trigger to help you recall other events from the trip. (If your memory needs additional refreshing, you always have that journal and box of pictures!) Limiting your image also helps make your goal attainable. Rather than looking forward to months, even years, of appliqué, by narrowing your focus you can realistically tackle the project, knowing an end is in sight. You will still have time to create all those other quilts you want to make!

CREATING A FILE FOLDER

Once you select a topic, make it official. Get a file folder and label it with a working title for your quilt. You now have a collection spot for ideas, thoughts, and the various and sundry items you will come across as you think about your quilt.

Often it's impossible to start on a quilt the moment inspiration strikes. Part of the enjoyment of creating a story quilt is being able to think about the subject over an extended time period. It's important, however, to have a place to collect your ideas so you won't forget them. Inspirations of one moment are often forgotten thoughts a moment or two later. Learn to take notes on scraps of paper or in a small notebook. Deposit your inspiration in the appropriate file folder at your earliest convenience.

When you see something in the newspaper, cut it out, and put it immediately into your folder. (If family members resent having the paper dissected before they read it, at least flag the page with a Post-it™ note.) I cut out articles that apply to the subject matter of a proposed quilt since I find they help me focus on my subject when it's time to create.

I also collect images as a starting point. Having something to look at or refer to as I draw can be helpful. A lot of printed matter besides newspapers comes into our homes. Of course magazines are a good source, but don't stop there. Forty percent of junk mail is never even opened. As you begin going through the day's mail, watch for glossy flyers advertising cultural events—they are often designed by graphic artists. You may come across interesting composition ideas as well as appropriate images.

COLLECTING QUILT BLOCKS

A quilt doesn't have to contain traditional quilt blocks to be considered a story quilt. However, building a quilt around one or two blocks is often a good starting place, particularly if you have only had experience making traditional quilts.

Since quilt blocks are part of our collective tradition, use quilt block names as a way of helping others decode your quilt's message. Start by looking at quilt compendiums, those marvelous collections of quilt blocks. If you don't own one, try your local guild or public library. (Consult the Bibliography for several titles.) In fact, many people get ideas for making quilts from just reading the list of quilt blocks in the index of a quilt compendium. If you're having trouble coming up with a topic, perhaps you could start here.

There are many appropriate blocks for most topics. Remember the list of questions you used when writing themes in school? "Who, what, when, and where." "Who" can be a person's name as well as a person-type like grandmother, sister, or bachelor. "What" refers to the specific subject of your story. For example, a travel theme might have you looking for airplane, railroad, or ocean blocks. Themes like friendship, patriotism, or even dishes would send you to different sections of your reference books. "When" could be the season of the year or the time of day, perhaps sunrise or end of day. All the states have state blocks that could be used for the "where." Many cities and countries also have their own blocks, or you could use simple directions, such as west. A little brainstorming and word association will get you going.

In fact, you will probably find more blocks than you can possibly use. Again, don't just create a sampler of appropriate blocks. It isn't necessary for you to use all the blocks you find, but it's nice to have a selection to choose from when your gathering process is complete.

Collect block names and designs in one sitting or as you go along. Look for additional ones as new quilt magazines arrive. In your leisure, go over the candidates and narrow the field. This is when you must seriously think about your skill level and time commitment. Many blocks are easy to draft once you know the basics of drafting. (For help in basic drafting, see Chapter 9.) A simpler version of a block often works just as well as a more complicated version and takes less time to make. Multiples can also be an important timesaving consideration. Remember, there's nothing wrong with creating or adapting existing blocks if you can't find suitable ones. That's how many blocks were added to compendiums, anyway.

As you will see, there are many ways to use quilt blocks in story quilts: singly or in multiples, as the major design motif or to form a background for other motifs, in the central design panel, or as borders. Blocks don't even have to appear on the quilt top, but instead can be used to enhance the back.

AMASSING A FABRIC COLLECTION

Some people are overwhelmed when they see too much new fabric. They don't know where to begin, or they consistently buy the same type of fabric over and over. They can only see their favorite colors or favorite types of prints.

Shopping for a story quilt will help you to view fabric in a different way. By having a "perceptual set" for specific categories of fabric, you can learn to broaden your selection. Once you've alerted your subconscious to be on the lookout for theme fabrics, you'll find they jump off the shelves at you. (You may discover some of your "finds" have been in stock for weeks. You just weren't ready to see them.)

An added bonus of working on a specific theme is that your friends will find fabrics for you, too. Jeanie Smith once placed an ad in *Quilter's Newsletter* asking for small pieces of car fabric in trade for a pattern of an Alaskan puffin. Years later, she still occasionally receives fabric in the mail because another reader has been poring over old issues of the magazine.

I often store my prints by subject, rather than color, so I have a large and diverse stack of "topic" fabric waiting when I'm ready to make my final fabric choices. If this final selection is going to work, there must be a number of good contenders to select from.

And I never feel guilty about buying a lot of fabric. It's the raw material of my creations. Having fabric in the house makes it possible to begin a quilt any time of the day, any day of the year.

SELECTING A COLOR SCHEME

I'll discuss specific color choices as we go along, but for now I'd just like to make a general comment about color, and present two specific color schemes.

By continuing the timeworn practice of making quilts color coordinated to match specific rooms in your house, you limit your creativity. How frustrating to have to leave out a thematically perfect fabric because it is the "wrong" color. Limiting your colors may also make it more difficult to express the emotions that go along with your subject. For story quilts, narrow your topic focus, but broaden your color range.

You may be concerned about what color scheme you're going to use for your quilt. How can you use so many different fabrics together? One possibility is a polychromatic color scheme. It contains all the colors from the color wheel, though they don't all have to be used in equal amounts or be rainbow bright. You can always emphasize certain colors by putting more of them in. Missing color steps between two prints can be filled in with nonsubject-matter texture prints, solids, plaids, or stripes. One way to grow in color usage is to expand your color scheme to a polychromatic color scheme rather than limiting yourself to only part of the color wheel. Many of the quilts in this book use this scheme.

A second possibility is a "pushed-neutral" color scheme which I first developed to use in decorative clothing (in my book *Wearable Art for Real People*). Basically, pushed neutrals means using soft, grayed variations of one or two hues combined with a wide assortment of grays and beiges. Value contrast is limited: there is no black or white because the contrast is narrowed to only part of the value range. The emphasis in the pushed-neutral scheme is on using both warm and cool versions of colors at the same time, and of not having everything match. Pushed neutral is about being subtle, but still having life in what is going on. Pushed-neutral schemes are particularly effective when used as background.

When a fellow quilter confided she was often disturbed by my use of the color yellow in my quilts, I replied, "That's right." Then she admitted she figured I had done it on purpose. Color is a tool. Just as you use traditional blocks to tell your story, you can use color to reinforce your meaning, to get your message across to the viewer. Be more adventuresome in your use of color. Stop limiting yourself to your favorite colors. Forcing yourself to add an "ugly" color may even make your favorite look better because it has a foil to see it against.

Some topics demand certain colors, and their use helps the viewer decode the quilt's message. Upon first viewing "Farewell to Mercy," a friend told me it was "frantic." (See Color Plate 16.) I worried about this overnight, and then phoned to ask what she had meant by her comment. She said that I had done a good job of portraying an over-whelming work environment. Design and color usage were responsible. I worked with a polychromatic color scheme, but the most obvious colors in the quilt are red, blue, and yellow, all equidistant on the color wheel. The resulting triad color scheme demands attention. The "frantic" images simply would not have had the same impact with soft, grayed colors.

Quilters coming from a home sewing background have been taught to over-match colors. They often wonder why their quilts seem lifeless. Nature uses all temperatures of color at once—both warm and cool. Just look at your garden! Rather than worrying about matching colors exactly, learn to buy from the whole fabric shelf. Don't stick to just one fabric line, but combine fabrics of similar but slightly different color from several lines. Their seemingly insignificant color variations will add life to your work.

My color class students know that when I describe their work as "quilterly," I'm telling them they have made a too predictable color choice. For example, if three corners of their block are green, so is the fourth corner. If three corners are medium value, the fourth one will be too. If a color appears on the right border of the quilt, it will most certainly make an appearance on the left, and probably at the top and bottom borders too! While these are all acceptable choices, they're also predictable and safe.

If you would like your color usage to expand, a story quilt is a perfect time to try something new. Use colors you have never used before, combine warm and cool versions of the same color, try a value gradation or color flow...your choices are unlimited.

"D" DAY

When "D" day—"Design" day—arrives, you will have a wealth of material to help you get started. Your folder will be crammed with blocks, images, articles, thoughts, and sketches. A pile of fabric will be waiting on the shelf to sift through. Rather than being overwhelmed by an empty design wall and a tablet of blank paper, you will have an assortment of materials at hand that will help you plunge into your new project.

Each of the 32 quilts featured in the following pages appears with its own story and at least one black-and-white photo. In addition, a color photo of each quilt appears in the Color Section (arranged in the same order as the stories). Throughout the discussion of design in Chapter 8, references are made back to the story pages, but do remember to also check the Color Section.

2. Remembering Childhood

Was your childhood ordinary, with a very small "o"? Before reading the stories and looking at the quilts in this chapter, you may have decided so. However, many of the quilters whose stories and work appear here have created quilts about experiences that probably weren't so very different from some of the things you did.

LEARNING TO ACCEPT OURSELVES:

"Make-believe Summer: At the Beach" by Mary Mashuta

You may want to work through parts of your childhood you didn't resolve the first time around as I did when I made my beach quilt in which I dealt with the problem of having pale skin in a beach-oriented society. Growing up is learning to accept who and what we are.

Photo 2-2. *Make-believe Summer: At the Beach* (detail). Photo by Jerry DeFelice.

MARY'S STORY

I grew up on Southern California beaches, manicured daily to the point of being almost unreal...a 300-mile paradise, with the sky filled with sun as the Pacific Ocean rolled in majestic waves at my feet...memories of salty, cool sea breezes and sand gritting in my swimsuit in all the wrong places.

In the days before sunscreens, filters, and blocks, "Tar Tan" was supposed to do the trick, but rarely did. The shame of the "sheet-white" body on a Southern California beach was almost more than this teenager could bear. Season after season, I exposed my redheaded peaches-and-cream complexion to the same ritual in a vain attempt to gain peer acceptance. Delicate skin, already out of fashion before my time, was nonetheless offered to the relentless sun. Coated in lotion, it soon scorched, and sometimes even blistered. All in the name of beauty. Each time the same cycle was followed—burn, ache, add a few freckles, and peel. Then try again....

Photo 2-1. *Make-believe Summer: At the Beach.* **Mary Mashuta.**
Photo by Jerry DeFelice. See also Color Plate 1.

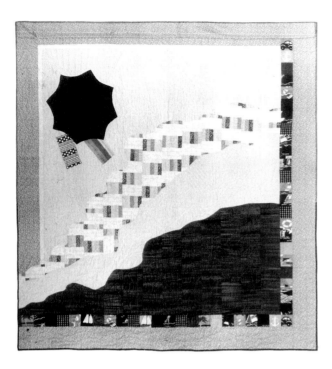

Photo 2-3. *Make-believe Summer: At the Beach* **(back). Photo by Jerry DeFelice.**

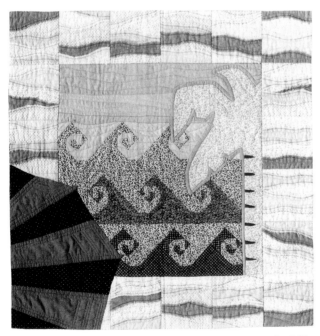

Photo 2-4. *Make-believe Summer: Under the Umbrella.* **36" x 36". Mary Mashuta, 1987.**

ABOUT THE QUILT

When I made "Make-believe Summer: At the Beach," I used the three figures to represent me: the first girl has a sheet-white body, the second has a sunburn, and the third sports the resulting freckles. Because the sun is so important to a beach society, I drafted a simple, stylized sun block which could be repeated in multiples. It was a wonderful opportunity to amass a "sun" collection of yellows, ranging from cool greenish-yellows to warm orange-yellows, and from small pin dots to large-scale dress fabrics.

Windblown Square blocks are used as filler in the sky. The blocks aren't noticed until the quilt is carefully studied. Quilts are more interesting when you can keep discovering new things to see as you approach them.

Creating an ocean allowed me to combine hand-dyed fabric from Japan, made by Akai Kawamoto, with other "water" fabrics in my collection. It was also fun to create a light source. It took me a long time to come up with the ocean block. Finally, the geometric ocean design knitted into a sweater caught my eye, and I realized I could adapt the Snail Trail block to create my own ocean block. (Patterns available for Mary's Ocean and Mary's Sun. See the Pattern Section.)

This was the first time I created a back for one of my quilts. I had a number of beginning items left over, and it seemed silly to waste them, so I designed an aerial beach view for the quilt back.

Later I made a second beach quilt, "Make-believe Summer: Under the Umbrella," which is smaller in size and less complex. This is a good example of applying the "less is more" principle if your quilt design is becoming too complicated. In it, I surrounded an ocean view with machine raw-edge appliqué block borders to represent the shifting sands of the beach. Hand appliqué would have taken a week; using this faster method, the blocks were completed in a day. More of this technique later.

Special Points
- Theme blocks
- Original sun block
- Block used as background filler
- Hand-dyed fabrics
- Light source
- Adapted traditional block to create new one
- Theme quilt back

Quilt Blocks

Mary's Ocean

Mary's Sun

Windblown Square

SCHOOL DAYS:

"Little Redheaded Girl" by George Taylor

We all remember parts of our childhood with a chuckle. George related such a story to me when he was a guest in my home, and I liked it so much, I even began a folder for him. He finally succumbed.

Photo 2-5. *Little Redheaded Girl.* **George Taylor. See also Color Plate 2.**

Photo 2-6. *Little Redheaded Girl* **(detail: twin needle machine quilting).**

GEORGE'S STORY

I attended a grammar school furnished with old-fashioned, combination desk/chair furniture. I sat behind the same girl in both first and second grades. She had red ringlets which kept falling across my desk and annoying me. At the beginning of second grade I warned her, "Keep it off my desk or I'll cut it!" She paid no attention, so I took a pair of scissors to her hair and presented her with one of the promised ringlets.

The next day she came to school with short hair! And, believe it or not, I was never punished for carrying through on my threat.

ABOUT THE QUILT

George wanted to use color to create a foreground and a background in his quilt. The ringlets, appliquéd in a variety of values and intensities of red, stand in front of the soft grayed pieced background. Eye-catching yellow-chartreuse scissors come even further forward visually. (It's not everyday you can work a neon color like this into a quilt.)

A draftsman by trade, George decided to enhance his theme by elaborating on an Ohio Schoolhouse block to create his own version of the central-tower, two-wing school to use in his background. (His sketch appears in Figure 8-24.) His pushed-neutral palette is made up of grayed peaches and pinks and a variety of grays and beiges.

George has successfully captured that "five minutes of your life" I mentioned earlier when I discussed selecting an appropriate topic for a story quilt. The piece speaks to us as viewers in a number of ways: it presents things to see at different viewing distances, it displays a sophisticated use of color; and, because the quilt is intriguing, we want to spend time decoding its story.

Special Points
- Foreground images
- Pieced background
- Neon color
- Theme block
- Adapted traditional block to create new one
- Pushed-neutral background

Quilt Block

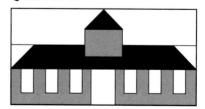

George's Schoolhouse

BIRTHDAYS:

"February 10th" by Karren Elsbernd

Were birthdays big events in your life when you were a kid? They sure were for Karren.

Photo 2-7. *February 10th.* **Karren Elsbernd. See also Color Plate 3.**

Photo 2-8. *February 10th* (detail: back).

KARREN'S STORY

February 10th is my birthday and hearts are very special to me, whether vibrant red, fancy pink, or modern magenta. As I was growing up, all of those Valentine decorations were for me and my day. I even wanted my birthday cake to be one of those in the bakery window decorated with lacy icing, hearts, and flowers. Then heart-shaped cake pans came

along, and my mother could make me pink heart-shaped cakes with pink frosting.

As a teenager, I would pick fragrant little bouquets of violets from our garden for my day. Woven into all of these childhood memories is a series of dresses. My mother shared her love of black-and-white fabric by making me these special dresses, each with different trims. I was particularly fond of white eyelet threaded through with black ribbon. Even today, all of these remain very special to me.

ABOUT THE QUILT

Karren decided to see just how frothy and sweet she could make her birthday quilt. She began by prominently displaying the symbols of the month—hearts and violets. Take note of the fading background pieced from the basket block called Cake Stand. The block is pieced first with strong value contrast between the individual pieces in the block; then the pieces in successive blocks become closer and closer in value so they blend together and are harder to distinguish. This design device helps draw in the viewer.

To add the memory of her dresses to the quilt, Karren designed two eyelet-trimmed borders. She created the threaded eyelet by using a combination of strip piecing, piecing, appliqué, and reverse appliqué. In addition to Karren's Eyelet, she also created appliqué patterns for Nosegay Ribbon and Violet Nosegay. (Patterns for all three are included in the Pattern Section at the end of the book.)

Karren has placed two hearts on the quilt back: a pieced one made from small squares and an appliquéd one. The latter she uses as her quilt label, noting the quilt name and her name, plus the dates she worked on the quilt.

As adults, we somehow seem to find less of a reason for celebration as our birthdays roll around. It's nice to remember it wasn't always so.

Special Points
- Theme block
- Background colored with fading effect
- Pieced background
- Original theme appliqué patterns
- Theme quilt label

Quilt Block

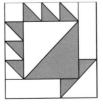

Cake Stand

FIRST TIMES:

"Let's Pretend" by Emma Allebes

Part of childhood is wanting to be a grown-up. But when do we actually grow up? Many Americans don't go through specific puberty rites; getting a driver's license as a teenager may be as close as some come to the rites of passage. However, there are other less spectacular events, like Emma's story, that can also serve as bridges to adulthood.

Photo 2-9.
Let's Pretend.
Emma Allebes.
Quilted by JoAnn
Manning. See also
Color Plate 4.

Photo 2-10. *Let's Pretend* (detail).

EMMA'S STORY

When memories from my youth come to mind, one of my favorites is recalling the joy I had every Saturday morning at 9 o'clock when "Let's Pretend" was broadcast on radio. One of the advantages of radio was my imagination was allowed to develop the characters of this wonderful fairy tale presentation.

A favorite of these stories involved a lovely Princess in a castle atop an icy hill waiting for her handsome Prince to win her hand if he could make it to the top, astride his mighty horse. Then there was the Good Witch of the North and the Wicked Witch of the West. Oh, so many wonderful memories!

One Saturday more than 40 years ago, when I was 12, my family was going on an outing. I asked if I could stay home, and it was agreed that I could. I had a secret mission to accomplish. I knew my father would not approve.

Just before 9 o'clock, I carefully placed a basin of hot soapy water on the floor in front of the radio. I then snitched my 19-year-old sister's razor. Last, but certainly not least, I switched on the radio to "Let's Pretend." There I was, shaving my legs for the first time—trying to grow up, but still content to hold on to childhood fantasies.

ABOUT THE QUILT

Emma has placed herself, gold lamé razor in hand, in the lower half of the quilt. A border print was cut up and pieced to represent the living room wallpaper and a wood-grained print was used for the radio. The wood-grained print appears again in a radio-shaped border that helps to unify the composition.

The upper reaches of the quilt are inhabited by Emma's favorite characters from "Let's Pretend." As a way of making her story a family experience, she decided to enlist the artistic talents of her grandchildren: the castle was drawn by ten-year-old Eric; the Prince, Princess, and hearts by five-year-old Madison; the radio by five-year-old Tierney. Notice the three-dimensional shark fins pieced into the water of the moat.

The radio show title and the slogan of its sponsor embellish the inner border. Musical notes are appliquéd above the radio and on this border. These visual cues serve to trigger memories in the viewer who also listened to the program. For those who didn't share Emma's experience, they add further hints to help decipher what is going on. If you plan to include words as visual cues, incorporate them into the overall design as Emma has done.

Special Points
- Lamé
- Theme-appropriate fabrics
- Grandchildren's artwork
- Dimensional shark fins
- Theme words

RITES OF PASSAGE JOURNEYS:

"Capezio Shoe-fly" by Mary Mashuta

My rites of passage included a nighttime train ride up the Central Valley of California when my sister and I went away to college. Also along on the train were trunks filled with bedding, clothing, and beautiful shoes, all packed in their own shoe boxes.

Photo 2-11. *Capezio Shoe-fly.* Mary Mashuta. See also Color Plate 5.

Photo 2-12. *Capezio Shoe-fly* (back detail: fabric photo pieced into Shoo-Fly block).

MARY'S STORY

When I was in high school, my mother had us practice budgeting by spending our allowance and earnings on our wardrobes. Since we made the majority of our clothing, the money was mainly spent on shoes. Capezio® shoes were the "in" shoe brand at our school, and it was impossible to own too many of these beautiful shoes.

Roberta and I had matching pairs of most of the shoes. However, there was only a single pair of palomino-colored dance oxfords which had been purchased on sale. A friend reminded me we spent our whole freshman year arguing over who would get to wear that one pair.

In the intervening years, I have grown to favor sturdy walking shoes. However, several summers ago I did see the magical word "Capezio" on a shoebox and the memories started flowing back to my teen and college years, when I was young and my feet never hurt!

ABOUT THE QUILT

After seeing the shoebox, I labeled a large yellow folder "Capezios" and began putting pictures of wonderful shoes in it. When Ann Boyce asked me to do a humorous take-off on a traditional quilt block for her "Humor in Patchwork" show, it was natural for me to select the Shoo-fly block.

To create a quilt background, I drafted three sizes of the Shoo-fly block. (See Figure 8-22.) Two sets of blocks were pieced in the soft beiges and grays of my pushed-neutral color scheme; one small-scale set was pieced in bold contrasting yellow and black. Then across the surface I tossed appliquéd shoes. It was fun to select not only the color of each shoe, but to also pick an appropriate lining. The bright, polychromatic shoes stand out against the grayed background.

On the quilt back (see Photo 8-4), I featured a dorm picture taken on my first night at the University of California. I think I look slightly overwhelmed. Wouldn't you agree? (To learn more about transferring photographs to fabric, see pages 66–69.)

Special Points
- Theme block
- Pieced background
- Pushed-neutral background
- Photographs on fabric

Quilt Block

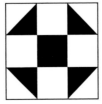

Shoo-fly

MEMORABLE EVENTS:

"The Devastating Hurricane of 1938" by Celia LoPinto

Natural disasters can leave lasting memories. Celia began the story quilt class thinking she had no tale to tell until she remembered a childhood hurricane.

Photo 2-13.
The Devastating Hurricane of 1938.
Celia LoPinto.
See also Color Plate 6.

CELIA'S STORY

To a twelve-year-old living in a small town, being sent home early from school seemed tremendously exciting. The rain had been heavy for about four days, the sky was threatening, and the wind was growing stronger and stronger. There was no problem making our way home in the rain since we had no school buses and always walked to and from school, dressed for the weather.

With no comprehension of the magnitude of the storm whirling rapidly past us, my sister and I stood awestruck and stared through the living room windows as trees bent and broke and leaves twisted through the air. My mother tried to keep as calm as she could to avoid frightening us. By the middle of the afternoon what we would later learn was a major hurricane had struck, cutting off all power on most of Long Island and throughout New England. There was no electricity in our town for three days—and so no radio to get reports on the storm's progress.

Although the storm had blown over by the next morning, information about what had happened was not easy to obtain. It was some time before our family learned that this hurricane had killed almost 700 people and caused $600 million in damage. Sustained winds went to 121 miles per hour and the peak gust in not-too-distant Rhode Island had been 186 miles per hour!

It is also interesting to note that this was before the Weather Service started giving names to hurricanes—so this one will always be referred to as "the devastating hurricane of September 21, 1938."

ABOUT THE QUILT

Celia has presented her story in an entertaining way which draws us into the quilt. The story unfolds in rows like a comic strip as we read the pieced block quilt from top to bottom. The upper portion represents what happened when the storm struck, and it is embellished with streaks of "beaded" rain.

In row four, the houses, windows, and sky become progressively lighter as the storm passes and electrical power is restored; a totally sunny house and vertical trees appear in the bottom row. A color dappled, blue-and-white abstract fabric represents the returning peaceful skies, and hand-marbleized fabric made by Sonya Barrington is used for a Sunbeam block sun.

For the back of the quilt, Celia devised a pocket to hold her story of the hurricane, the story of the quilt, and photocopies of the *New York Times* for the days after the storm. Celia returned to the scene of the quilt story and photographed her school, then included this image (transferred to muslin) along with a photo of her parents' home on the quilt label.

Special Points
- Reads like comic strip
- Theme blocks
- Embellished with beads
- Theme-appropriate fabrics
- Hand-marbled fabric
- Back pocket with documentation
- Transitional border blocks

Quilt Blocks

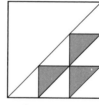
Birds in the Air

Celia's Schoolhouse

House

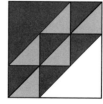
North Wind

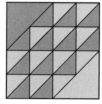
Ocean Waves

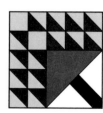
Pine Tree

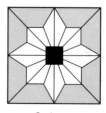
Sunbeam

3. Family Stories, Tales, and Memories

Do you treasure a special story about someone in your family? This kind of story makes your family more real to you, and repeating the story over and over makes it belong to you more. Why not pass along the story to the next generation of your family through a story quilt?

FAMILY TRIPS:

"Westward Ho!" by Mary Mashuta

Journeys are a part of life. Americans move around a lot—opportunity always seems to be lurking around the next corner. The most monumental event of my childhood was the journey that brought my family out west. In 1984 I wrote about our trip, and five years later made my quilt for the California Heritage Quilt Project's "Road to California Quilt Contest."

Photo 3-1.
Westward Ho!
**Mary Mashuta.
See also
Color Plate 7.**

MARY'S STORY

I remember a childhood journey undertaken from New York to California, the land of oranges and golden opportunity. The time was shortly after World War II. The cast of characters included my 1940's pioneer-style parents, a gunmetal gray Plymouth coupe, and five-year-old girls, carbon copies of each other. A sleek, streamlined Alma trailer served as our contemporary Conestoga wagon.

Before our eyes a nonstop ribbon of asphalt unraveled daily. Other images blur, except for those of giant rocks piled precariously like baby's blocks, and gargantuan cactuses, their arms stretching skyward.

Years later, we tried to determine how long this seemingly

endless journey actually lasted. Calculated in child-time, it must have taken at least six months. My mother, when closely questioned, said, "Yes, it was a long time. I'm sure it took at least six weeks!"

ABOUT THE QUILT

I saved my story in a folder labeled "Trip to California." I collected pictures of cactuses and desert scenes, and added photo essays of cactuses and buildings taken when I visited Arizona and New Mexico. I even made an abstract collage in an art class which proved a vital step in helping me make my final design more abstract.

For the sky in "Westward Ho!" I used a print from a children's fabric collection that reminded me of a Georgia O'Keeffe painting. An assortment of objects float through my sky in a surreal way—lopsided squares with holes in them represent the view from my car window, nine-patches made of biscuit puffs represent clouds, and there are of course saguaro cactuses. Compare the two pictures from the Arizona photo shoot with my fabric interpretation which is embellished with quilting designs and one-inch origami puffs tied with quilting thread. Strips of origami puffs were also repeated in the desert below.

To create my desert blocks, I decided to make random raw-edge appliqué blocks again. This time, instead of using soft, flowing curved edges as I had done in the beach quilt, I cut zigzags and straight edges. The designs painted on a Santa Fe doorway served as my inspiration. (To learn more about raw-edge appliqué, see Chapter 9.)

I knew the quilt would be an opportunity to use and enjoy the large collection of subtle, mostly solid pushed-neutral fabric I had amassed to represent the desert. To create a pleasing color flow, I arranged my fabric in color-coordinated stacks going from rust-beige all the way to green-beige. Individual blocks and borders could then be composed. The borders were also built around four different-colored monotones of a trip photo. (The border is discussed further on pages 75 and 76.)

"Westward Ho!" was certainly a long time in coming, but I enjoyed thinking about and collecting for the quilt over the years. Sometimes the journey, and not the destination, is the goal.

Photo 3-2. Saguaro cactus detail. Photo by Mary Mashuta.

Photo 3-3. Taliesen West: Saguaro Cactus Theme. Photo by Mary Mashuta.

Photo 3-5. Santa Fe: Painted doorway. Photo by Mary Mashuta.

Photo 3-6. *Westward Ho!* (detail: desert).

Photo 3-4. *Westward Ho!* (detail: saguaro cactus).

Special Points
- Photo essays
- Collage
- Traditional biscuit puffs
- Origami puffs
- Embellished with quilting thread
- Raw-edge appliqué blocks
- Pushed-neutral color scheme
- Photographs on fabric
- "Southwestern" fabric on back

REMEMBERING MOTHERS:

"Emma's Eggs" by B. J. Welden

B. J. remembered a humorous memory of her mother, affectionately called Emma, to depict in her story quilt.

Photo 3-7.
Emma's Eggs.
**B. J. Welden.
See also
Color Plate 8.**

Photo 3-8. Fabric with chicken shape cut out.

B. J.'S STORY

During World War II we were encouraged to do our part for the war effort by planting vegetable gardens—called victory gardens. My father decided to also raise chickens in a coop under the back porch to further our contribution to the cause. Anyone could go and collect the eggs, except my mother. I'm convinced those chickens knew my mother's footsteps—and they would all gather at the door awaiting her arrival—she'd open the door and they would all fly out. We'd have to get all the neighborhood children to go out and capture the escapees and return them to the coop.

ABOUT THE QUILT

In "Emma's Eggs," B. J. depicts her childhood backyard with the victory garden planted in the foreground. The remaining ground is filled in with Hen and Chickens blocks, pieced in low-contrast pushed-neutral beiges. The sky over the back fence has also been pieced in a theme block: Birds in the Air. The house siding was made from a wood-grain print; the screen doors of the coop, from a Japanese *yukata* print; the interior coop space, from a large-scale black-and-white photo-realism floral print which looks like shadows.

The egg-gathering commotion is in full swing with Emma bustling into the coop as unhappy chickens flutter around the yard. In the photo of the fabric detail, you can see how B. J. achieved the effect of the feathers on her chickens by carefully cutting portions of a large-scale southwestern print which contained feathers. It is easy to be overwhelmed by large-scale prints and forget to look at the parts which make up the whole. To learn to appreciate the possibilities this type of prints offers, cover a print with a sheet of typing paper that has a small hole (several inches wide) cut in it. With the majority of the print masked, you see only a small portion. Move the paper across the surface and see what comes into view.

B. J. has enjoyed collecting '30s and '40s fabrics at antique shops and flea markets over the years. She used one of the vintage fabrics for her mom's dress. Appropriately, to finish her piece, B.J. made an egg-shaped quilt label.

Special Points
- Theme blocks
- Pushed-neutral color scheme
- Specialty prints
- Large-scale prints
- Vintage fabrics
- Theme quilt label

Quilt Blocks

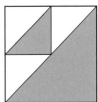

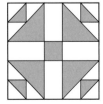

Birds in the Air   Hen and Chickens

COMMEMORATING FATHERS:

"Fritz's Dimond Roller Rink" by Barbara Dallas

Barbara was able to recall many wonderful memories of her father, her teen years, and the roller skating rink he owned as she made her story quilt.

Photo 3-9.
Fritz's Dimond Roller Rink. Barbara Dallas. See also Color Plate 9.

Photo 3-10.
Fritz's Dimond Roller Rink (detail).

BARBARA'S STORY

The quilt came out of my memories of my father's skating rink and all the happy times I had there as a teenager. I guess this quilt is really a tribute to him—he was known and loved by so many people. He had a real understanding of young people and helped more than one who had gone astray.

The rink was located in the Dimond district of Oakland, California, where the MacArthur Freeway now stands. It was a very sad day for our family when the building was razed to make way for the freeway. For a long time my dad couldn't go anywhere near the area.

Skating began for me at the age of thirteen. My brother and I skated in several statewide competitions in skate dancing. You could also take proficiency tests in dancing for bronze, silver, and gold medals. Over my skating "career," I made dozens of skating skirts and dresses. We skated to the music of 78 rpm records, drank gallons of soda, and had lots of fun.

I have come to realize that this quilt has taken on a special and unexpected meaning for me. In the later years of my dad's life, it became impossible for him to care for himself and we were forced to switch roles as parent and child. For a long time these were my last memories of him. In working on and planning this quilt, I was transported back to a much happier time that my dad and I shared together. Now when I think of him I remember a happy, energetic man filled with enthusiasm. I know he would be pleased if he could see my quilt.

ABOUT THE QUILT

While making the quilt, it became fun for Barbara to recall the details of skating life and find ways of turning them into images she could machine and hand appliqué onto her background which was pieced from three beige fabrics. It is a real joy for the viewer to stand in front of the quilt and devour the minutiae. Look at her cola bottles. They needed to be transparent so she stacked six layers of tulle and zigzagged them together at the edge after inserting brown fabric underneath to represent the beverage. She even made a dimensional skate key for her rental clip-on skates.

To add show business glitz, Barbara embellished the quilt with sequins. An Art Deco border represents architectural motifs used in the skating rink building. (The border is discussed further on page 76.) She even worked in a theme fabric on the quilt back which didn't seem to fit on the front—a good way to make use of the excess, leftover fabrics you've collected specifically for a story quilt. (See it in Photo 8-23.)

Special Points
- Three-fabric background
- Transparent bottle
- Novelty fabrics
- Dimensional skate key
- Embellished with sequins
- Art Deco border
- Theme fabric for back

LIVING WITH HUSBANDS:

"One Arm Bandit"
by Bonnie Bucknam Holmstrand

Recycling has always been a part of quiltmaking. Bonnie's husband, Mark, unwittingly contributed fabric for a project in a class taught by my sister. The leftover fabric and incident became the raw materials to create a story quilt.

Photo 3-11. *One Arm Bandit.* Bonnie Bucknam Holmstrand. Photo by G. Craig Freas. See also Color Plate 10.

Photo 3-12. *One Arm Bandit* (detail). Photo by G. Craig Freas.

BONNIE'S STORY

For a Roberta Horton "Plaids and Stripes" workshop in 1988, I needed to expand my fabric collection, since I didn't have a good selection of plaids or stripes. I found a bunch of my husband's dress shirts in a trunk in the garage which I assumed he had set aside for charity. I cut the right sleeve off of all of them to take to the workshop. Mark saw me come in from the garage and asked what I was doing with his shirts. I explained that I was collecting some fabric for the workshop. The upshot was, they were not shirts he was going to give away. He was losing weight and the shirts were part of his wardrobe he was moving back into!

ABOUT THE QUILT

Bonnie decided it would be only right to use the leftover shirts to make a quilt in my story class. While discussing design possibilities, I had mentioned that sometimes the parts of things are more interesting than the whole. Bonnie began by sketching individual shirt parts. It quickly became apparent she could develop simple repeat units, so she drew a series of quilt sketches that recombined the basic units in various ways. (See her sketches in Figures 8-5 through 8-10.)

All of Bonnie's shirt and sleeve blocks were made from Mark's shirts. The detail shows the large shirt in the center portion of the quilt. When the shirt was appliquéd in place, the collar and tie were left three-dimensional. Some of the shirt pieces are held in place by stitching on top of the actual tailored top stitching. Bonnie has embellished the piece with additional buttons.

To make the background negative space more interesting, Bonnie pieced it in two-inch pushed-neutral beige and gray squares. She even managed to subtly work in several airplane blocks to symbolize Mark's hobby of building and flying radio-controlled airplanes. (See Figure 8-10.) Quilted scissors show up well against the shirts and background.

Special Points
- Actual shirts and tie
- Embellished with buttons and labels
- Pushed-neutral background
- Theme blocks
- Scissors quilting pattern

Quilt Blocks

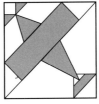

Airplane

One-patch

FAMILY PETS:

"Smokey the Cat: Rescue at Midnight" by Mabry Benson

Do you have a favorite family story involving a beloved pet? It is fun to plan a quilt around one of these stories. Smokey the cat became a member of Mabry's family in 1973 and was still around in 1990 when she created her quilt about him.

Photo 3-13.
***Smokey the Cat:
Rescue at
Midnight.***
**Mabry Benson.
See also
Color Plate 11.**

MABRY'S STORY

Smokey sticks close to home. If he is out when someone is away, he shows up at the door when they come home. We were surprised when we didn't see him at the front door after being out for the night. Nor did he show up when we came home from work and school. This was not like our cat. I tried calling, but no Smokey. Periodically I went outside and called again, but I heard nothing until 9 o'clock, when I heard a faint meow. By this time it was already dark, and Bill wasn't coming home until late. The meowing was coming from the cemetery that's in back of our house. I followed the sound until I was under one of the redwood trees. Shining the flashlight up into the tree, I found Smokey, rather high up. I went home and got a can of cat food to try to entice him down, but that didn't work.

When Bill came home around midnight, he got out the tall ladder. We carried it over to the cemetery, and he climbed up the ladder to get the cat. Smokey didn't appreciate the effort and climbed higher up the tree. I returned home for a bag to stuff the reluctant cat into as I didn't want Bill to fall off the ladder trying to hold him. I also got the camera to record the rescue. Finally, armed with the cat food and bag, Bill tried again and was able to coax Smokey close enough to grab and "rescue" him.

ABOUT THE QUILT

Mabry has used an interesting composition to tell her story. Her tree has been paper-cut and fills the center of the quilt. For a more intimate composition, some of the branches have been cropped, rather than letting them extend to their full length. This device pulls one in and makes the viewer a part of what is going on. As in children's and folk art, the size of details is determined by narrative importance rather than actual real-world size. The story is about Smokey, so he gets to be big. Supporting details like the gravestones and ladder are smaller.

It can be difficult to portray a nighttime scene in fabric. If you only thought "green" for a tree, your search for fabric candidates would be limited. For Mabry's tree, she selected a Hoffman tropical leaf print colored in blue-green, gray, and black! The unexpected coloration was a perfect choice when the tree silhouette was stitched in place. The color and "leaf" feeling are much more important in expressing "nighttime tree" than whether the fabric really looks like the needles of a redwood tree. It is easy to be too literal in the translation of personal images into fabric. Translating the essence and feelings of the story is what is important.

Mabry had to search for a suitable fabric to use for the flashlight beam. It was difficult to find something sufficiently transparent: most voiles were too reflective and shiny. Finally she located a transparent polyester voile that was easy to see the background scene through.

Mabry has chosen to piece a nighttime sky with the Milky Way block rather than using a one-color solid background. By sticking to a narrow color range of blue, blue-violet, and purple solids and monotone prints she has made the sky far more interesting. Complexities such as this keep on rewarding the viewer with more and more to see as the quilt is approached.

Special Points

- Paper cutting
- Cropping
- Scale distortion
- Nighttime color scheme
- Theme print
- Specialty fabric for flashlight beam
- Pieced sky
- Theme block
- Words

Quilt Block

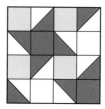

Milky Way

4. Work Experiences

Mark Twain said, "Work consists of whatever a body is obliged to do.... Play consists of whatever a body is not obliged to do." If work's no fun, why make a quilt about it? Well, we all do it, even if we receive no monetary reward for our efforts. Why not celebrate work you love, comment on work you consider to be drudgery, or say good-bye to work you no longer do?

HONORING WORK:

"Hanky for the Teacher" by Mary Mashuta

At the end of her life, my mother bravely fought illness. I wanted to say so many things that were hard for me to verbalize; I wanted to ask so many questions I never got around to asking. In 1988, I did take action and made a quilt to honor her and her life's work.

Photo 4-1. *Hanky for the Teacher.* **Mary Mashuta. See also Color Plate 12.**

MARY'S STORY

"Hanky for the Teacher" was made to honor my mother and all the good things about teaching. It has nothing to do with grading papers, giving tests, and sitting in teachers' meetings. It's about the excitement of helping others to learn and opening their eyes to the world around them.

When I was a child, students often gave their teacher a hanky or candy as a holiday present. My sister and I always knew what were in the boxes, especially the flat, square boxes, when she brought them home. Crisply folded, many of those hankies were passed on to us when we went away to college. Over the years they have remained as tangible proof that someone was there.

The hankies became useful "useless" tokens of appreciation—elegant, dainty carry-overs from another time tucked away in satin and lace cases tied with dainty ribbons. The small squares of delicate, fine fabric had personalities just like the students who offered them—quiet, timid, sweet; flamboyant, extroverted, demanding. Each pupil added to the group character of his or her class. Children standing and sitting in well-ordered rows in old photographs...some faces well remembered, others long forgotten...each class contributing to a canvas that when completed becomes a life. Many small parts, but like a patchwork quilt, eventually composing a whole creation to stand back and admire: a life's work. Much more than the sum total of paychecks issued. Countless days spent nurturing, encouraging, coping. A legacy passed on to her daughters by example set.

Photo 4-2. Temple City: Mrs. Mashuta's third-grade class.

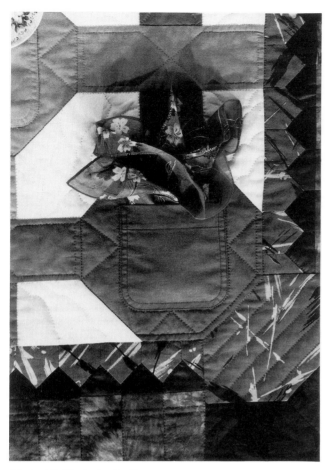

Photo 4-3. *Hanky for the Teacher* (detail: pocket with hanky).

ABOUT THE QUILT

The quilt gave my mother and me something positive to discuss in phone conversations. She unearthed her stash of "class" pictures, annual documentation of how she earned her living. She also spent time looking for her favorite "teacher" photograph of herself. It was incorporated into the quilt back (see Photo 8-5).

Since I wanted to actually use the hankies, I had to find some way to incorporate them into my quilt design. While looking at school-related blocks, I came across Tile Puzzle. It was an interlocking grid design containing octagon-shaped pieces. I added pockets to the octagons to hold the hankies and renamed the block Hanky Puzzle. To make the repeat block format more interesting to compose, I added a color flow across the grid and played with atmospheric changes in the negative space. Since the quilt concept was a gift to my mother (she didn't want any more material possessions), I also got the idea to place a symbolic ribbon around the quilt and tied it with a Bow block. (See my quilt sketch in Figure 8-16. The pattern for the Bow block is included in the Pattern Section at the end of the book.) Later I created Crayon blocks to

be pieced into the ribbon. Quilt friends gave me hankies to add to my own collection so I was able to select ones to complement the color flow of my grid. A closeup detail of one of the pockets, with a hanky from Japan, is shown here.

When the quilt was completed and photographed, I gave a set of color prints and the duplicated story to Mother. She enjoyed sending these to some of her teacher friends. When she died, we hung the quilt at a gathering of her friends, and each person was given a copy of the story printed on schoolroom-green paper. I also sent photos and stories to faraway relatives and friends. This was not something I had planned on doing when I made the quilt; it just seemed right at the time.

I am glad I made "Hanky for the Teacher" to honor my mother. The quality time we spent discussing the planning is treasured, and the hours I spent designing, sewing, and quilting while I thought about her were marvelously well spent.

Special Points
- Photograph on fabric
- Actual handkerchiefs
- Theme blocks
- Color flow grid

Quilt Blocks

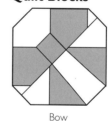

Bow

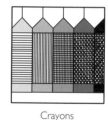

Crayons

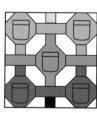

Hanky Puzzle

HUMANITARIAN WORK:

"Someday May They All Be Free" by Leslie Hatch-Wong

You may find you want to make a story quilt to celebrate the work of a member of your family. Leslie wanted to honor her husband's humanitarian work as a doctor when she planned her story quilt.

Photo 4-4. *Someday May They All Be Free.* Leslie Hatch-Wong. See also Color Plate 13.

Photo 4-5. *Someday May They All Be Free* (label).

LESLIE'S STORY

In my quilt I tried to reflect a vision of stories I had heard whenever my husband Doug returned from his work in Africa. Much of his work was with refugee families in Sudan, or with refugees forced by civil war in Mozambique to flee to the neighboring country of Malawi.

Refugees never voluntarily leave their farms or ancestral lands, but move because they are trying to avoid the brutality of armed civil conflict in their homelands. Unfortunately, this scenario has become increasingly common over the past few decades, and there are now millions of refugees in Africa. After Doug returned from his work at several of these locations, he said that despite the unspeakable poverty, hunger, and death suffered upon these people, there was an amazing amount of hope. Parents forced to trek across long distances, often with no food, money, or possessions, never seemed to lose their love for their children or pride in their cultural heritage. The hope of freedom always seemed to empower refugees to take incredible risks.

ABOUT THE QUILT

The layout of a symphony brochure gave Leslie an idea of how to arrange and compose the parts of her quilt. She used the Star of Hope block to piece together a desert landscape. In the foreground she decided to place camels in a desert scene to symbolize Africa and the Sahara. When it came time to draw her camels, Leslie had difficulty finding pictures to use as models so she suffered through endless drawings. Just after she completed her final sketches, the Sunday paper arrived with the missing pictures! Both Leslie and I found them too late to be of any help. (Months later I was *still* finding camels for her.)

Leslie had brought some of Doug's beautiful photographs to class and wanted very much to build her quilt around them. She selected a grouping of mother and child pictures to arrange across the sky. She enlarged the color prints into color photocopies and had them transferred to beige fabric.

To frame her scene, Leslie pieced a repetitive, but ever-changing border from fabric she had purchased in Bali, Indonesia. Although her quilt is monochromatic in coloring, it is rich in feeling because she has varied her values and introduced interesting prints.

She completed her quilt with a dedication on the quilt back. Doug is pictured in Malawi with a Mozambique refugee child perched on his knee.

Special Points
- Theme block
- Photographs on fabric
- Specialty fabrics
- Theme label

Quilt Block

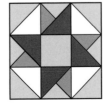

Star of Hope

UNASKED-FOR WORK:

"Ladies of the Board"
by Janice Ohlson Richards

Although Jan has long considered herself a serious quilter, she had never thought of herself as a career woman. But then things changed.

Photo 4-6. *Ladies of the Board.* **Janice Ohlson Richards. Photo by Ken Wagner. See also Color Plate 14.**

Photo 4-7. *Ladies of the Board* **(detail). Photo by Ken Wagner.**

JANICE'S STORY

Seven years ago my two sisters and I, due to our father's retirement and other family circumstances, were thrust into the position of serving, along with my brother, on the board of our father's custom millwork company, "Coastcraft." The company had been singularly managed in the same location for sixty years and has really been a part of the family's history! But we were raised in the generation when a woman's place was in the home: my sisters and I had always been totally isolated from the business. Aside from being full-time home-

makers, our other interests were in traveling, golfing, quilting, knitting, and volunteer and club work. Suddenly finding myself one of the "ladies of the board," I can only remember feeling apprehensive, worried, and totally over my head! Trying to learn (or understand) the millwork business monopolized much of our time, but we learned to make decisions and work with new people. It definitely drew the three of us together.

As our tenure on the board was coming to an end, I felt compelled to design a quilt as a tongue-in-cheek response to our unexpected dilemma of serving on a company board. This quilt would serve as a memory of the years we worked together.

ABOUT THE QUILT

Jan's design is centered around Coastcraft with its jagged factory roof line. Neutral colors depict the dull tones of the aging business, basically unchanged from day one in appearance. Jan made a series of Attic Windows blocks, piecing several of the plaid windowpanes to indicate broken glass and deterioration. Surprisingly, she found two other traditional blocks to use in constructing her building that would be appropriate to the millwork business: Millwheel and Board Meeting.

The fun began when it was time to dress the cast of characters sitting at the board table. The sisters' attire is not necessarily appropriate to the boardroom. Lift the polka-dot skirt, and you'll find Jan's plaid golf shorts! Looking at her leather golf shoes and ribbed knit socks, it's obvious where she's been. Jan says, "The colorful feminine legs under the table give hope for a bright future, with all the feet soon to be planted firmly on the ground."

Special Points
- Theme blocks
- Dimensional clothing
- Nontraditional fabrics

Quilt Blocks

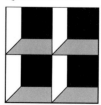

Attic Windows   Board Meeting   Millwheel

UNUSUAL WORK:

"Lucy Flagbody Goes Fishing" by Jeanie Smith

Today women are employed in many jobs which would have been considered out-of-the-ordinary just a generation ago. I knew Jeanie had previously worked on state road crews flagging, but the Alaskan "fish" story is a bonus.

Photo 4-8. *Lucy Flagbody Goes Fishing.* Jeanie Smith. See also Color Plate 15.

JEANIE'S STORY

When I was a flagger I was called Lucy Flagbody by the crew. One summer I was flagging in the Turnagain Pass Rest Area which is about seventy miles south of Anchorage. Over a period of a week, one man had repeatedly regaled me with his fish stories while he waited in stopped traffic. I always countered by asking him when was I going to get my fish. Well, as luck would have it, the day the fisherman planned to make good on his boasts, I had to flag him through. As he sped by in his car, I heard my name yelled out as the hand from an extended arm tossed a brown paper bag at me. Inside I found a cleaned, freshly caught silver salmon. I had caught a fish thirty miles from the nearest salmon hole!

ABOUT THE QUILT

Jeanie has arranged her work gear on an abstract print background that gives the feeling of swirling dust. After countless years of collecting "road" fabrics, she selected two to use for her hard hats. Check out the laced work boots. Her theme continues into the borders: the Delectable Mountains block is pieced for two adjoining ones; fish appliquéd to paper-bag-like fabric circle the other two. No quilt is complete without a back. Her friends urged Jeanie to buy an eye-catching neon orange-and-chartreuse fish print for hers. (Enjoy it in Photo 8-24.)

Jeanie gave herself a special fortieth birthday present. After twelve years of flagging, she quit! In a bizarre footnote, the woman who was Jeanie's flagging partner just happened to drop by the room where Jeanie was taking the story quilt class. They hadn't seen each other in years!

Special Points
• Theme fabrics
• Dimensional shoelaces
• Theme blocks
• Theme fabric for back

Quilt Block

Delectable Mountains border

Photo 4-9. *Lucy Flagbody Goes Fishing* (detail).

LEAVING A JOB:

"Farewell to Mercy" by Mary Mashuta

In 1984, I decided it was time to leave my teaching job and become a full-time quilter. Like Jeanie ("Lucy Flagbody"), I gave myself a birthday present and handed my resignation in during March. I then began toying with the idea of creating some kind of quilt about my years at the school. In the end, I began planning a going-away quilt for myself.

Photo 4-10. *Farewell to Mercy.* **Mary Mashuta. See also Color Plate 16.**

MARY'S STORY

"Farewell to Mercy" symbolizes my leave-taking from twelve years of frantic teaching in a parochial school, Mercy High in San Francisco.

Twelve years of toil depicted on a quilt. Twelve years of dawn risings in a frigid house to cross the Oakland–Bay Bridge for another day in the classroom. Twelve years of papers graded, page by page, line by line, and word by word. Countless bran muffins, heaping portions of macaroni and cheese, gallons of tea sipped a cup at a time, all swallowed and gone forever. Nuns serving in ever-diminishing numbers, adding a quiet, loving dignity. A dedicated staff, all working for the best, but often at cross-purposes. Every June a class of

sophisticated graduates; in August a batch of eager freshmen. I outlasted many, but not all. No more fashion shows coordinated, garments graded, finals proctored, and tests scored. No more delicious freedom when it was all over for another year....

ABOUT THE QUILT

I put my feelings down in words, but once I had officially graduated, the story wouldn't take a quilt-like form for me. I didn't do the scale drawing until the following fall. When it did come out, it emerged rapidly and full-blown. Only minor changes were made after that. Some story quilts just seem to have a protracted gestation period.

In the meantime, I began collecting appropriate fabrics and quilt blocks: Sailboat because the students were known as the Mercy Skippers, Wind at Sea because teachers are long-winded, and Streak of Lightning to symbolize the big and little problems connected with any job.

In the central panel, Monopoly-like houses are stacked on hills just as you would see them in San Francisco. My paper doll folded cut-outs of Mercy girls streak across the sky. They are cut from a plaid fabric as close in appearance to the Mercy uniform plaid as I could find. I had assumed the girls would occupy one of the borders, but finally realized they were too important to relegate to such a position. Now they float in the sky, above all the turmoil below.

I reverse appliquéd leave-taking words into the borders, and cross-stitched one of the lines of my story with DMC® Perle cotton thread and waste canvas as further embellishment.

Special Points
- Theme blocks
- Paper doll folded cut-outs
- Theme fabrics
- Reverse appliqué words
- Cross-stitched words
- Theme fabric for back

Quilt Blocks

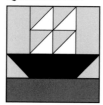

Sailboat

San Francisco House

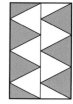

Streak of Lightning

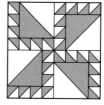

Wind at Sea

FINDING A NEW CAREER:

"I Just Want to Make Red Shoes"
by Lynn Brown

I made a quilt when I left teaching; Lynn made one as she prepared to enter teaching. Lynn had a high-pressure job that paid well, but for quite some time she had wanted to make a career change. Then one night she had a dream that changed her life.

Photo 4-11. *I Just Want to Make Red Shoes.* **Lynn Brown. See also Color Plate 17.**

Photo 4-12. *I Just Want to Make Red Shoes* (detail).

LYNN'S STORY

I am dreaming...I find myself tossed into deep water of the sea. I notice that I don't feel fearful of being there, as I would be if I were not dreaming. I am very familiar with my surroundings, but I am angry at finding myself there. I am bobbing around in the water shouting, "I don't want to be here, I just want to make red shoes!" I shout this over and over again, and I can see images of red shoes made of soft grainy leather, with little ties on the toes.

When I woke up from the dream, I was fortified with a resolve to change my career in a direction that would allow me greater creativity and would allow me to do something that I want to do. That very day I went to the clinic and quit my job; then I went out and bought myself a pair of soft red shoes.

I too quickly chose another job that was a mistake as far as creativity was concerned, but this time I quit after three weeks. I have since decided to become a teacher, at the secondary level, of Spanish and of English as a Second Language.

ABOUT THE QUILT

Lynn used the Wild Waves pattern to piece the central panel of her quilt. Since she hadn't worked in prints in several years, she had to begin a campaign of "water" hunting. She found it particularly challenging because she was creating so many different types: deep mysterious water, slow moving murky water, and both crashing and choppy waves.

Because of her new "south of the border" focus, Lynn decided to frame her water panel with appropriate design motifs: the top inner border is called Aztec Towers, the lower inner border has Aztec-style fish, and the outer border uses Aztec Rays. The placement of the cloud fabric enhances the dream-like quality of the piece. Here she has also scattered her notorious red shoes.

Special Points
- Theme blocks
- Color study of water
- Theme motifs
- Theme fabric for back

Quilt Block

Wild Waves

5. Coping with Life

Not everything that happens in life is happy, but coping is one of the ways to become truly human. Making a quilt about the hard times can help one to get through them and go on. The quilters in this chapter have shared a very intimate part of their personal life with me, and now, with you. I thank them for not only making their quilts, but also for having the courage to share their stories.

NATURAL DISASTERS:

"Quake of '89" by Mary Mashuta

On October 17, 1989, Americans had the chance to witness the first live, nationally televised earthquake as a 7.1 "big one" struck Northern California. Crews were on hand to televise the World Series, and before we knew it, big-name news anchors were flown in to add their interpretations of what was going on. The world sat in its armchair spellbound and watched the painful drama.

Photo 5-2. *Quake of '89* (detail).

MARY'S STORY

Having escaped personal injury and property damage in the Loma Prieta Earthquake, I nonetheless felt a close bond to those who were suffering in areas close by—not half a world away. Most Northern Californians were in a state of collective shock, going around in a stupor, glued to our television sets for hours on end.

I hadn't planned on making an earthquake quilt. However, early the Saturday after the quake, I said to myself, "Why not?" I went into my studio and worked until 11:30 that night. The energy of creation was a heady thing to experience.

This was a golden opportunity for me to try and capture what I had witnessed and felt, to try to regain control of my life. As art therapists will tell you, we take control by being able to make decisions that can be carried out. I could decide how large my quake was going to be by determining my quilt size; I could decide what color my quake should be by picking colors from the fabrics still piled neatly on my shelves; I could decide what to include in my quake by coming up with my own design.

Photo 5-1. *Quake of '89*. Mary Mashuta. See also Color Plate 18.

Photo 5-3. *Quake of '89* **(back).**

I worked mostly from the fabrics in my own collection though a friend shared decorator-weight abstract cottons to help me complete my vision. Using a few, I completed the front, and had leftovers for the back. When some of the prints were juxtaposed, the picture they presented seemed so grisly, I couldn't bear to use them together. I literally got goose bumps. For that reason, I took the fabric with the computer-generated running people and put it off by itself.

Since I had commuted on the Bay Bridge for twelve years and could see the damaged section from my sister's window, I decided to feature it on the quilt back. I cut apart a large zigzag print which looked like the double-decked bridge and staggered it in sections down the back. To document the quilt, I used my computerized Bernina® to write the earthquake's name and vital statistics. (See a detail in Photo 8-18.)

The following October, just one year after the quake, I coordinated a gallery show of earthquake quilts and garments made by many of us who had experienced—and coped with—that memorable day. (Articles about the "Quake of '89 Show" appeared in several quilt magazines. They are listed in the Bibliography.)

Special Points
- Hand-dyed fabrics
- Theme fabrics
- Theme block
- Decorator-weight fabrics
- Theme quilt back
- Writing with sewing machine

Quilt Block

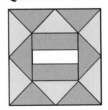

End of the Road

I wanted to feature the Marina District fire in San Francisco because I had taught at adjacent Fort Mason the preceding summer. I also had commuted on both the Bay Bridge and Cypress Overpass, two structures severely damaged by the quake. Though many other areas of the state had been devastated (Santa Cruz, for example), I knew my quilt—my quake—would center on the areas I knew best.

ABOUT THE QUILT

I began by adapting a drawing I had saved in a "house" file to represent the Marina buildings with their windows on fire. Above the houses, I added triangles of hand-dyed fabrics made by Debra Lund, Nancy Clemmensen, and Akai Kawamoto. These were perfect for my flaming sky because of their colors and abstract flowing designs. I filled out the design area with prints, plaids, and paisleys, sticking pretty much to a red-orange palette. I came across a quilt block called End of the Road and knew it could be pieced with car fabric and staggered to represent the collapsed Cypress Overpass. I serpentined the blocks across the lower quilt front.

NEAR ACCIDENTS:

"Incident at Harris Ranch" by Beverly Karau

Some of life's journey's end in unforeseen ways. Bev and her husband live in the Central Valley of California and have their own small plane; all three became important cast members in an unexpected drama.

Photo 5-4. *Incident at Harris Ranch.* **Beverly Karau. See also Color Plate 19.**

Photo 5-5. *Incident at Harris Ranch* (detail: cotton field in perspective).

BEV'S STORY

Harris Ranch is a restaurant on Highway 5, on the way to Los Angeles. It has an airstrip and we like to fly in for dinner periodically. One evening we flew our Cessna in for a nice peaceful dinner and in the process hit the nearby unlighted power lines. We were very lucky and didn't exactly crash, but settled down into the cotton field at the end of the runway. No one was hurt but the plane was damaged and unflyable. The FAA ruled that it was an "incident" rather than a crash. I'm not sure why—maybe because no one was injured, for which I am exceedingly grateful.

ABOUT THE QUILT

Bev decided to go for a simple quilt to commemorate the incident. She selected Aircraft and Cotton Reels blocks to tell her story. To make her quilt composition more interesting, however, Bev presented the scene in perspective. (For a discussion of the process, and to see her preliminary drawings for the quilt, see pages 70–72.)

Bev located a brown-and-white remnant that reminded her of cotton puffs and combined this with a number of other prints and a plaid to represent the cotton field. She also found star prints in a variety of sizes to represent her night sky. The largest stars are appliquéd on as circles. She couched metallic cording to represent the power lines.

Rather than signing her quilt in the usual way, Bev embroidered both Larry's and her signature and the date of the "incident."

Special Points
- Theme blocks
- Blocks in perspective
- Theme fabrics
- Couching

Quilt Blocks

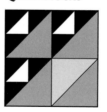
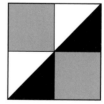

Aircraft   Cotton Reels

WORKING THROUGH NEGATIVE EXPERIENCES:

"Hong Kong Blues" by Kay Sakanashi

I knew Kay had her wallet stolen on a recent trip, and when she enrolled in a story class, I suggested she tackle the subject of the wallet to "get the bad taste out of her mouth." She almost abandoned the project given the feedback she got from home ("you shouldn't make a quilt about such a negative thing"), but she persevered and in the process turned a painful experience into something worthwhile.

Photo 5-6. *Hong Kong Blues.* **Kay Sakanashi. See also Color Plate 20.**

KAY'S STORY

I had a wonderful trip to Japan on a quilt tour; additional days were tacked on for a side trip to Hong Kong. The trip was marred, however, because I had my wallet stolen.

The narrow streets of Hong Kong were teeming with bodies. My cousin and I were busy poking into one store after another. All of a sudden I looked into my purse and no wallet. I checked all the pockets, inside and out, and we retraced our footsteps. No wallet. Even though I had been warned about pickpockets, I said to myself, "It couldn't happen to me." But it did and I was in shock. The police were no help. They just

looked at me and shrugged their shoulders. "Nothing we can do." I thought of the credit cards and license that would have to be replaced. Part of my identity was gone. I had been violated, even though I wasn't physically hurt.

ABOUT THE QUILT

Kay had recently completed a color class with me, and could use the quilt as an opportunity to do a color study using what she had learned. She had an interesting design approach: she began with a collage made from magazine photos and wrapping paper, then proceeded to a glued mock-up, and finally tackled the actual quilt. (See these and get more details of the process on pages 74 and 75.)

Kay's small quilt is a jewel. She found three traditional blocks that seemed particularly appropriate: Fool's Puzzle, Rob Peter to Pay Paul, and Crosses and Losses. She chose the latter as her background block. Using a wide variety of black and gray solids and prints, she has moved from a dark value, sinister lower portion to a lighter value, more ethereal upper portion.

Over the background field, Kay lay the items that tell her story. At the bottom, hands clutch a silk purse, used symbolically to stand for her wallet. Red lightning bolts emphasize the bad deed. In an upper golden shaft of light, a miniature purse and real money ascend skyward to the never-never. Kay has slashed the composition diagonally with a serpentine band of real sashiko stitching done in the Rob Peter to Pay Paul pattern. It symbolizes the Japanese part of her trip or the fact that she is Japanese-American, whichever you prefer.

Alas, life is not always sunshine and light—it has its darker moments. Happily for Kay—and us—her story quilt brought some value out of her negative experience.

Special Points
- Color study
- Collage
- Glued mock-up
- Theme block
- Embellished with real purses and coins
- Theme sashiko embroidery

Quilt Block

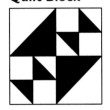

Crosses and Losses

UNDERSTANDING WHAT IS MEANT TO BE:

"Release" by Deanna Davis

Deanna shares a touching story dealing with a mother's love. When her son dropped out of school at age sixteen, Deanna turned to quilting for comfort. She kept track of the development of her quilt "Release" by writing daily notes as it evolved. Let's re-read her journal with her later thoughts added.

Photo 5-7.
Release.
**Deanna Davis.
See also
Color Plate 21.**

DEANNA'S STORY

SATURDAY, JAN 28. *Had to get out of house today. Cotton Patch [quilt store] as far as I could think to go. Found ABC fabric and picked out primary colors for a big schoolhouse quilt. ABC fabric triggered idea of starting the quilt....*

I remember leaving the fabric store quite excited about all the clear bright colors I was planning to use. By the time I reached home I was absolutely frantic to get started. I started cutting and cutting through the colors I love so much, all the clear reds, greens, and blues. Then I was slashing and ripping bright pieces of color...and standing in front of my pinup board, weeping and raging. It was really scary. I kept shredding fabric and pinning and pinching that poor schoolhouse until it turned skinny and mean and ugly and all the color disappeared and became that horrible purple I hate!

Finally I calmed down enough to sit down and grab a piece of paper and pencil. I wrote "schoolhouse" in the middle and then all the rage and grief and anger words came shooting out from it. My son's name...and how special and wonderful he is...the devastation school had brought to his life. Finally I understood what this quilt was trying to help me say and I could work with it instead of fighting it.

SUNDAY, JAN 29. *Something weird is happening...It's turned into a wall quilt...Used Mary Mashuta's technique of writing ideas and key words. "Let me out of here" led to explosion of design out upper corner. Vine and big flowers to signify John's strength and beauty...Worked late.*

MONDAY, JAN 30. *Up early. Figuring this out! I'm making a mourning quilt for all the frustration and sadness that led my gifted son to leave high school at age 16. Quilt celebrates his strength and uniqueness and sings of his wonderful future.... Bed at 2 a.m.*

TUESDAY, JAN 31. *Worked a very long time today.... Explained quilt to John, i.e., my sadness and anger at schools. He was interested. He and I stayed up until 3 a.m. Oh God he is finally talking to us.*

I swear the day I explained this quilt to my son is the day he started to recover from his depression. If it was okay for Mom to be so mad and sad and frustrated, it was okay for him, too.

WEDNESDAY, FEB 1. *Up early...Realized the ABC fabric is the million teacher grades making their rigid evaluations according to their standards....*

FRIDAY, FEB 24. *Bev brought by fabric samples. With these I was able to add final bits to schoolhouse quilt. Could have made more beautiful and complicated...but have decided it's supposed to be more like a cartoon—not a Flemish flower masterpiece. The design is not to look right but be jarring and unsettling....*

ABOUT THE QUILT

Deanna used fabric, color, and words to work through a difficult time in her life. The quilt packs an undeniable emotional wallop.

Having a quilting background in which she had studied color and design gave Deanna the necessary tools to build her quilt, even if she didn't always feel she was in control of what was going on. This quilt happened spontaneously and didn't involve much conscious preplanning. The important thing was Deanna went with the gut level feelings that "directed" her about what to do. She had the strength to remain open to what was happening before her eyes and to ride out the experience.

Special Points
- Journal
- Spontaneous design
- Theme fabrics
- Theme appliqué block

Quilt Block

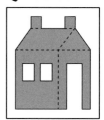

Deanna's Schoolhouse

LOSING LOVED ONES:

"Sunset at Mazatlan: The Beginning of Tomorrow" by Peggy Johnson

Mourning quilts are a part of quilt history. After Peggy saw some examples in class, she realized she could give herself permission to undertake the difficult task of making a quilt about a personal loss.

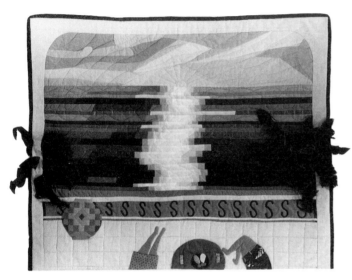

Photo 5-8. *Sunset at Mazatlan: The Beginning of Tomorrow.* **Peggy Johnson. See also Color Plate 22.**

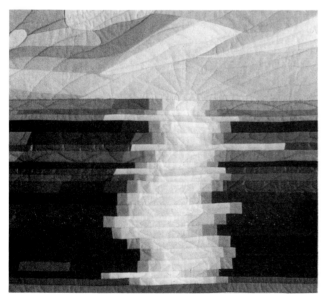

Photo 5-9. *Sunset at Mazatlan: The Beginning of Tomorrow (detail).*

PEGGY'S STORY

My story is one that seems to be happening more and more these days. We had two daughters killed, two years apart, by drunk drivers. Needless to say, I experienced a lot of trauma, and due to the nature and the results of these accidents, I was left very bitter and depressed. I went through what everyone goes through when one's children are killed in a violent act. I had a lot of guilt: I blamed myself and everyone else. Though this was normal, it was very hard to go through.

My husband and I decided to go on a trip to Mazatlan to get away for awhile. At sunset one day, sitting on the deck talking, it finally came to me that I had to live with this for the rest of my life and that I had to accept it. I couldn't do anything for my girls but one thing, and that was be the kind of person they would be proud of. I vowed to be a more kind, thoughtful, tolerant, and understanding person. This revelation opened up the way for me to see more clearly and to begin to heal.

I was thrilled when Mary asked me to make this quilt. I wanted to do it, but dreaded opening up old wounds. But the more I progressed on the quilt, the better I began to feel. It seemed to help me remember all the love, the laughter, and good times we had shared together. It also made me realize that whenever I look at this quilt, I will be able to renew my vow and each sunset will be my "beginning of tomorrow."

ABOUT THE QUILT

The moment on the balcony was the image Peggy selected for her quilt. We see a partial, aerial view of the couple. Peggy appliquéd them and the wrought-iron balcony railing in place but decided to make her vegetation three-dimensional. After a number of attempts, she finally glued and machine zigzagged wire between two fabric leaves and then clipped them to create the palm fronds that suggest the tropical setting.

The sunset sky was appliquéd, but Peggy experimented with strip piecing to create the path of the sun across the ocean. For her, the sunset became a beginning rather than an end.

Special Points
• Dimensional vegetation
• Strip-pieced ocean

6. Vacations and Travel

Have you ever had a vacation that was too good to believe? Are you planning a trip now? Why not plan a quilt about your travels? You may ask, "But how do you collect a specific spot and turn it into a quilt?" There are many ways to "see." You can photograph, sketch, or do color studies. You can always buy books, postcards, and fabric! All these can help you be more aware of what you are seeing, and the more of your senses you personally involve, the more real the experience will be for you later when you begin your quilt. Don't even worry about coming up with a specific image—that can, and will, come later after you are home.

FOREIGN FABRICS:

"Gaijin" by Mary Mashuta

There's nothing like new and different fabrics to inspire me. I have purchased Japanese fabrics for years, but when I went to Japan I still felt compelled to add to my collection. My favorite find was a Japanese Boys' Day banner. The banners are hand painted, but mass-produced, in factories. To me it was a great textile artifact.

In addition to looking for fabric finds in Japan, I also took photo essays and observed social customs which helped to imprint the country on my mind. This is all recalled when I look at my quilt.

MARY'S STORY

Foreign travel can afford an opportunity to practice a new set of etiquette. Children born into a society are socialized into the customs and think little about them. Sensitive visitors, wishing not to offend and be thought of as rude, often make vain attempts to do what is "proper," even though it may make little sense to them because they were schooled in a different set of accepted practices.

In Japan, I learned to switch from "street" shoes to "house" slippers upon entering a home. Should a trip to the bathroom be necessary, I had to change to "WC" slippers...and, of course, back to the "house" slippers upon leaving. A person beset with constant allergies, I was cautioned against blowing my nose in public. I enjoy talking with my hands, but I was told not to point. It's hard to keep from being considered rude when there are so many new things to exclaim over and point out.

While out shopping one day, my sister and I stepped right up to the bakery counter to make our purchases, totally unaware the shoppers had formed a line to wait their turns. The Japanese, in their politeness, only scowled dragon faces at us...but said not a word. Realizing our blunder, we tried to apologize and bow. On the inside, however, we wished the floor in front of the counter could open and gratefully swallow our red, embarrassed, tall, freckled bodies.

Photo 6-1. Detail: Japanese Boy's Day Banner. Photo by Mary Mashuta.

Photo 6-2. *Gaijin* (detail). Mary Mashuta.

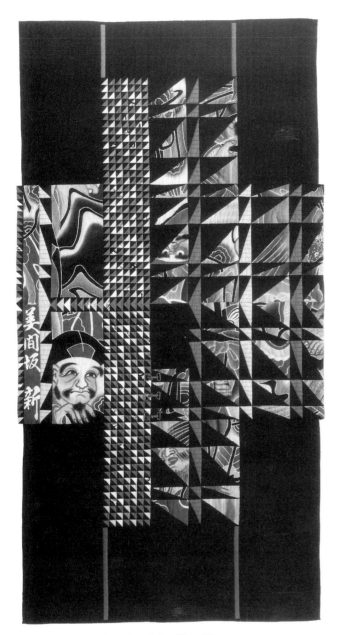

Photo 6-3. *Gaijin*. See also Color Plate 23.

ABOUT THE QUILT

Upon my return, I was asked to do a piece for a kimono-inspired show Marinda Stewart was coordinating for Quilt Festival in Houston, Texas. Luckily for me, the challenge fabrics were compatible with my banner. Rather than using a kimono shape for my basic quilt design, I used the simpler shape of the *michi yuki haori,* an over-garment for the kimono. I decided to do away with the side seams and open the entire garment out flat. To make the garment area more interesting, I used a contorted grid made up of squares divided into triangles for my design surface. (For a sketch and discussion of the process involved, see Figure 8-11.) I even embellished the garment front with metal toggles purchased in a crowded, many-box notions store. (And for a look at the back, see Photo 8-25.)

To introduce some of the colors found in the banner, but not present in the challenge fabrics, I added blue, orange, and khaki beige to the one-inch triangles seen grouped in the wide band running the length of the garment. The khaki bridged the distance between the true green Marinda had given me and the dirtier green in the banner. When colors don't go together or match, keep on adding intermediary colors until they do, rather than removing the offending ones.

I didn't select a specific storytelling image to portray my story. The name "Gaijin" became appropriate for my quilt because I viewed the Japanese textile I used as only a foreigner would. (It became another example of not fitting in.) Japanese quilters would see it as inappropriate, a throw-away item; they would prefer to use their family silk kimonos or new commercial quilt fabrics for their quilts.

In 1987, I coordinated a gallery show of quilts, "Gaijin: American Quilters Visit Japan." Articles about the show appeared in several quilt magazines. They are listed in the Bibliography.

Special Points
- Ethnic Japanese fabric
- Photo essays
- Observed social customs
- Contorted grid
- Embellished with found objects
- Machine-tucked fabric

We had proved we were foreigners because we offended, by merely being us—American born and bred. We weren't "ugly" Americans, purposely being uncouth, unknowing, and little caring. We had conscientiously made an effort to be the perfect ambassadors, but we were unschooled in the Japanese book of etiquette. With so little effort on our parts, we truly had become gaijin, a word politely translated today as "foreigners" though literally meaning "white devils."

FOREIGN IMAGES:

"Feasts and Facets: Memories of Portugal" by Judy Sogn

Sorting trip memorabilia provides a good starting point for a quilt. Judy found a travel poster that got her started on designing a quilt about her recent trip to Lisbon, Portugal.

Photo 6-4. *Feasts and Facets: Memories of Portugal.* **Judy Sogn. See also Color Plate 24.**

Photo 6-5. *Feasts and Facets: Memories of Portugal* (back detail).

JUDY'S STORY

I have many images in my head of Lisbon, but most of all, Lisbon is buildings stacked picturesquely on hills. One of my favorite buildings was a sixteenth-century house studded with facets. I also loved the intricate tile sidewalks.

As an American woman accustomed to the use of washers and dryers, I was fascinated with the laundry seen hanging from many windows. While this is picturesque, I would still rather have my washer and dryer!

It was hot when we were in Lisbon and my husband and I enjoyed treating ourselves to "Feast" ice cream bars in the afternoon. After a refreshing pick-me-up, we were ready to tour some more and soak up the sights of the city.

ABOUT THE QUILT

Judy replicated her Portuguese travel poster city scene in machine piecing, insetting many areas rather than fracturing the walls into more easily pieced units. The scene was drawn on poster board and cut apart to become templates. Sewing was a real challenge, but Judy is sure she can machine piece almost anything now. To finish the scene, she appliquéd a boat in the harbor.

Surrounding the main scene are four different borders that gave Judy an opportunity to picture additional, supportive themes. The facets from the house are pieced in the top border. Four gradations of a hand-dyed fabric were used to create an optical illusion of depth.

The ever-present laundry is featured on a side border. Remembering that "less is more," she used four simplified pant shapes to represent the laundry. For the other side border, she grouped ice cream bars. Decorative tile sidewalks are represented in the final, lower border. The word "Lisboa" is set into a black-and-white checkerboard to give a tile effect. (For a discussion of designing theme borders, see pages 75 and 76.)

For the quilt back, Judy selected the only print in the quilt, a simple landscape that suggests the Portuguese countryside. She followed the sidewalk theme when she made her quilt label.

Special Points
• Machine pieced and appliquéd scene
• Theme borders
• Theme fabric for back
• Theme quilt label

FAMILY VACATIONS:

"Sierra Getaway" by Kathleen Dimond

Kathy wanted to celebrate wonderful family vacation memories in a quilt. She finally decided to concentrate on the skiing she and her family enjoy so much.

Photo 6-6. *Sierra Getaway.* Kathleen Dimond. See also Color Plate 25.

KATHY'S STORY

My husband, children, and I have been skiing the Sierra for years now. My teenage daughter and preteen son started skiing when they were four years old and have progressed from whining toddlers to fearless terrors on the slopes. Now they sometimes wait for us at the bottom of runs.

The trip always begins with the congested traffic at the Benicia Bridge. We head for the mountains in our Dodge Caravan in the afternoon daylight and usually arrive at the lake as the stars come out. Some trips are a breeze—others have been through unforgettable snowstorms.

We've had many getaways, stayed in many different cabins, and skied all over. We most often go the north end of Lake Tahoe travelling over Donner Summit where we watch the train rambling through the mountains. We also enjoy the nightlife in the casinos at the south end of the lake.

Brilliant sunny days, crisp mornings, goodie bags filled with lemon drops and candies, frozen toes, lost mittens, close friends, thrills, spills, races, follow the leader, centipedes, jumps! Skiing has it all for family fun.

ABOUT THE QUILT

Kathy made a serious commitment to making her quilt, and it grew and grew as she worked on it. She included seven different pieced blocks by the time she finished the large top: this is quite a feat, and I wouldn't recommend it to any but the most hearty. Kathy says, "Just getting all the different blocks to fit was a challenge." (She even hid

Snowball and Nine-patch in the snow!) Many of the blocks required expert piecing as they were quite small. For instance, the Snail Trail blocks, which make up the varied waters of Lake Tahoe, are only three-inch blocks.

Kathy was able to fit in abundant appliquéd details from the getaways. She used the zigzag stitch to machine appliqué her pictorial work, but first she fused the pieces in place for more control.

Photo 6-7. *Sierra Getaway* (label). Note cross-stitch snowflakes.

Special Points
- Theme blocks
- Machine appliqué
- Theme label

Quilt Blocks

Delectable Mountains border

Evening Star

Pyramids

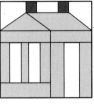

Schoolhouse

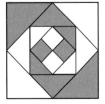

Snail Trail

Snow Crystals

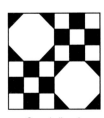

Snowball and Nine-patch

SPORT TRIUMPHS:

"Look But Don't Touch" by Elizabeth Aneloski

Liz also made a sport-related quilt, but in addition, it's about overcoming a personal limitation.

Photo 6-8. *Look But Don't Touch.* **Elizabeth Aneloski. See also Color Plate 26.**

Photo 6-9. *Look But Don't Touch* (detail).

Photo 6-10. *Look But Don't Touch* (computer generated fabric label). **Photo by Mary Mashuta.**

▶

LIZ'S STORY

My husband and I, together with a group of scuba diving friends, planned a diving vacation to Bonaire. After we paid for the trip, I (being a nondiver) decided I wouldn't be able to take full advantage of the trip unless I learned to dive. Somehow snorkeling didn't seem to be enough, so I took scuba diving lessons from a close friend who's a dive instructor. He patiently taught me, step by laborious step (good thing, because I was far from a natural). After slow progress and much handholding, I became comfortable underwater, and discovered what a wonderful world there is beneath the ocean's surface.

ABOUT THE QUILT

To depict the tropical locale of her island off the coast of South America, Liz divided her central pictorial panel in half: ocean surface and sky above, an underwater scene below. A giant diving mask is superimposed over the panel and acts to divide the two scenes.

Liz found special underwater and fauna print fabrics in Bonaire that lent themselves to her theme. A hand-marbleized fabric worked well as the ocean. To differentiate the ocean surface (as seen through the mask) from the underwater areas, she covered the portion below it with a translucent sheer fabric. The fabric adds a mystical quality to the scene.

To hold her underworld fish and fauna in place, Liz resorted to shadow appliqué. Individual pieces were first stitched between the sheer and water fabric with metallic or colored thread applied in a decorative pattern. Later she outlined the individual motifs with white quilting thread as the piece was quilted. Liz discovered it was necessary to overcompensate with bolder fabrics if she wanted the colors to show through the sheer.

To complete the composition, Liz used silk-screened prints made by Katie Pasquini Masopust: stars in the sky, flamingos in the border.

LOOK

BUT DON'T TOUCH

JUNE 1990

ELIZABETH ANELOSKI

Special Points
- Theme fabrics from locale
- Hand-marbled fabric
- Translucent sheer overlay
- Shadow appliqué
- Silk-screened fabric

1. *Make-believe Summer:*
   At the Beach
   1987. 75" x 81"
   Mary Mashuta
   Berkeley, CA
   Photo by Jerry DeFelice

2. *Little Redheaded Girl*
   1990. 41" x 31"
   George Taylor
   Anchorage, AK

3. *February 10th*
1990. 41½" x 37"
Karren Elsbernd
San Francisco, CA

4. *Let's Pretend*
1990. 44½" x 64½"
Emma Allebes
Fair Oaks, CA
Quilted by JoAnn Manning

42

5. *Capezio Shoe-fly*
   1988. 44" x 55"
   Mary Mashuta
   Berkeley, CA

6. *The Devastating
   Hurricane of 1938*
   1990. 48" x 48"
   Celia LoPinto
   San Francisco, CA

7. *Westward Ho!*
1989. 72" x 81"
Mary Mashuta
Berkeley, CA

8. *Emma's Eggs*
1990. 39" x 46"
B. J. Welden
Kensington, CA

9. *Fritz's Dimond Roller Rink*
   1990. 54" x 54"
   Barbara Dallas
   Moraga, CA

10. *One Arm Bandit*
    1990. 58" x 62"
    Bonnie Bucknam Holmstrand
    Anchorage, AK
    Photo by G. Craig Freas

11. *Smokey the Cat:*
    Rescue at Midnight
    1990. 34" x 41"
    Mabry Benson
    Kensington, CA

12. *Hanky for the Teacher*
    1988. 72" x 81"
    Mary Mashuta
    Berkeley, CA

46

13. *Someday May They All Be Free*
1990. 48" x 56"
Leslie Hatch-Wong
San Francisco, CA

14. *Ladies of the Board*
1990. 68" x 40"
Janice Ohlson Richards
Vaughn, WA
Photo by Ken Wagner

15. *Lucy Flagbody Goes Fishing*
1990. 40" x 61"
Jeanie Smith
Anchorage, AK

16. *Farewell to Mercy*
1986. 56" x 71"
Mary Mashuta
Berkeley, CA

17. *I Just Want to Make Red Shoes*
1990. 62" x 72"
Lynn Brown
Chico, CA

18. *Quake of '89*
1989. 43½" x 57½"
Mary Mashuta
Berkeley, CA

19. *Incident at
Harris Ranch*
1990. 44" x 69"
Beverly Karau
Prather, CA

20. *Hong Kong Blues*
1990. 24" x 30"
Kay Sakanashi
Richmond, CA

21. *Release*
    1989. 39" x 44"
    Deanna Davis
    Piedmont, CA

22. *Sunset at Mazatlan:*
    The Beginning of
    Tomorrow
    1990. 56" x 38"
    Peggy Johnson
    Sequim, WA

23. *Gaijin*
1986. 48" x 90"
Mary Mashuta
Berkeley, CA

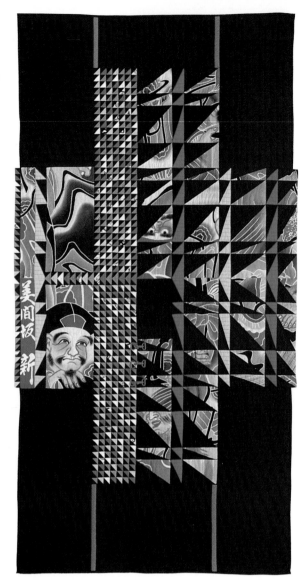

24. *Feasts and Facets:*
Memories of Portugal
1990. 30" x 41"
Judy Sogn
Seattle, WA

25. *Sierra Getaway*
1992. 70" x 73"
(unquilted top)
Kathleen Dimond
Lafayette, CA

26. *Look But*
Don't Touch
1990. 30" x 39½"
Elizabeth Aneloski
San Ramon, CA

27. *The Colors of Vegas*
1990. 58" x 43"
Charlene Phinney
Puyallup, WA

28. *Coming to Terms* (Side 1)
1990. 60½" x 60½"
Mary Mashuta
Berkeley, CA

29. *Exodus: April 1942*
    1990. 44" x 38"
    Donna Egan Holt
    Billings, MT
    Quilted by Margie Hay

30. *Letting Go*
    1990. 46½" x 57"
    Naoko Anne Ito
    Berkeley, CA

31. *Minor Inconveniences*
1990. 60" x 60"
Bonnie Bucknam Holmstrand
Anchorage, AK
[From *Fit to Be Tied*
by Judy Hopkins,
That Patchwork Place, Inc.,
Bothell, WA, 1989]

32. *Ivory Is for Elephants*
1990. 54" x 54"
Barbara Dallas
Moraga, CA

BUSINESS TRIPS:

"The Colors of Vegas" by Charlene Phinney

Charlene probably had the best of both worlds: a business trip that would be classified as a dream vacation by many quilters. She attended a Mary Ellen Hopkins Seminar in Las Vegas, and while she was too busy sewing to participate in the casino scene downstairs in the hotel, she did observe it.

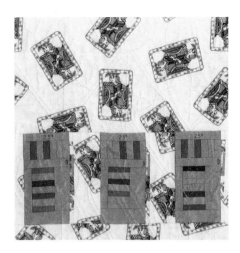

Photo 6-13.
The Colors of Vegas
(back detail).

Photo 6-11. *The Colors of Vegas.* **Charlene Phinney. See also Color Plate 27.**

Photo 6-12. *The Colors of Vegas* (detail).

CHARLENE'S STORY

The colors of Vegas are those of golds and tans—sun and people. People that pivot around the slots and games, like a herd of cattle milling around a water trough or salt lick. The kind of mindless feeding of big machines that open and swallow and open again. The belch that sends out a few coins, then the rush of the crowd to see what's happened. You stay to feed it again, never ending, never changing. Feed—pull—wait—feed—pull—wait—feed—pull—wait....

ABOUT THE QUILT

Charlene did a simple sketch in which she used slot machine mouths and coins to symbolize the gambling scene. She scattered four mouths across the quilt's central panel: one tips over into the border. The design device of having images from the center panel enter the border helps to keep the activity going.

The quilt background required only one template: a simple obtuse triangle which could be alternately flipped. The resulting zigzag lines also add to the activity level of the piece. Charlene selected a wide assortment of prints and solids to further reinforce the gaiety and confusion. Notice how she placed darker value triangles around the quilt edge to create an optical border.

To complete the gambling theme, Charlene embellished the borders with gold, make-believe coins and did the machine quilting with metallic thread. Three quick-pieced slot machines are added to the quilt back. They are just waiting for our quarters.

Special Points
- One-template piecing
- Value change creates border
- Embellished with coins
- Metallic thread for machine quilting
- Theme back

7. Social Commentary

Have you ever felt helpless about what was happening in the world around you, felt one voice wouldn't make a difference? This section provides a written and pictorial record of quilters who decided to speak about the world they lived in, who designed and made quilts that go well beyond being "warm and cuddly."

COMMENTING ON WAR:

"Coming to Terms" by Mary Mashuta

"Coming to Terms" was made in 1990, before the sending of troops and the resulting war in the Persian Gulf. It is a Vietnam War quilt, and as such, it also reflects the place we were historically before the Persian Gulf War. Further, I had to work with then-available fabrics; the plethora of patriotic fabrics available as the anniversary of Columbus' voyage approached was not yet available. In 1990, I had to work around the Jesse Helms' "flag-and-art" controversy; by 1991, flags were everywhere in our culture. Americans couldn't get enough of American flags.

Photo 7-2. *Coming to Terms* (side 1). **Mary Mashuta. See also Color Plate 28.**

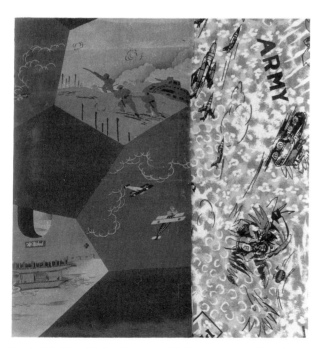

Photo 7-1. **War fabrics: Japanese silk kimono scrap, American cotton.**

MARY'S STORY

Vietnam was my generation's war. I experienced the war from the home front as I listened to the daily battle statistics on the local FM radio station. (The droning voice of the

announcer is forever imprinted on my mind.) Other Americans preferred a ring-side seat as they sat in front of their television sets and made the six o'clock news part of their evening meal. It was no longer necessary to go to the local theater for prepared newsreels of war coverage; the footage was daily, immediate, and in color.

There are more than two sides involved in a war, even though that's all it takes to fight it. In the Vietnam War, an ever-growing third group was the Peace Movement. I was part of that group, an average, ordinary citizen back home who couldn't comprehend why my country was sending the men of my generation to a war halfway around the world.

I wanted my war quilt to speak about this duality: to speak about those who because of their patriotism went to fight the war, and of those, equally patriotic, who took a stand and said we shouldn't be fighting the war. If a quilter ever needed a two-sided quilt, this was the time. "Coming to Terms" was not an easy quilt to create. It was just one I had to make.

Photo 7-3. *Coming to Terms* (side 2).

Photo 7-4. *Coming to Terms* (detail: side 2. "Peace Rally" photo.)

ABOUT THE QUILT

For years I collected fabrics: I looked for jungle fabrics and added more patriotic red, white, and blue selections to my 1976 Bicentennial collection. "War" fabrics, like those pictured, also came my way. (Can you imagine wearing clothing made from either one?) I had service photos of men from my life transferred to fabric, ready to add. I

patiently collected quilt block ideas, looking for the perfect one. My thoughts jelled for the quilt front after finding the block Patriot's Quilt. To be able to showcase more fabrics, I divided the parts of the continuous block into more pieces and renamed it Vietnam Patriot's Quilt. (For a discussion of the process, see page 70.)

I wanted to play my two categories of fabric against each other: jungle against red, white, and blue. The grid created by the block would be a perfect format. From afar the photos on fabric don't particularly stand out; they only become apparent as the viewer approaches and is drawn into the quilt.

The back, which was to represent the Peace Movement, was harder to design because I had to deal with the flag image I had always planned to have there. I had collected sketches of waving American flags and even purchased several inexpensive printed ones from a local quilt shop. To me the flag was a symbol which needed to be included in my quilt, but how realistic should, or could, I be? After Jesse Helms, realism seemed out; a stylized flag would work better.

I also wanted to represent how the life had gone out of Vietnam after years of conflict. I did this by using four jungle fabrics in the center area: the first has all the bright colors intact, the second has been reduced to monotone green, the third has become a faded khaki, and the fourth is Mabry Benson's nighttime tree fabric. This time it symbolized the "dead" terrain.

"Coming to Terms" is probably as far away from a pretty quilt as I'll ever make. I find viewers bring themselves and their own experiences to the viewing of the quilt; they see beyond what I thought I was putting in it. I have been told "It's rigid and yet chaotic at the same time...just like war," and "It's disturbing in a compelling way."

Special Points
- Theme fabrics
- Hand-dyed fabric
- Ethnic Japanese fabrics
- Photographs on fabric
- Theme block
- Theme back
- Embellished with peace badge

Quilt Block

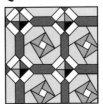

Vietnam Patriot's Quilt

HISTORY AS VIEWED BY AN OBSERVER:

"Exodus: April 1942"
by Donna Egan Holt

For many of those who lived through the Second World War, the horror and heartbreak of war took place here, in our own "free" country. Let's look at two quilts that deal with the particularly wrenching event of the internment of the Japanese Americans: one made by an observer, one made by a participant.

Donna was upset because she had nothing special to write in a "memory" book for her grandchildren. In a story class she realized she did have something to share, something from her childhood she wanted them to know about.

Photo 7-5. *Exodus: April 1942.* **Donna Egan Holt. Quilted by Margie Hay. See also Color Plate 29.**

DONNA'S STORY

In the spring of 1942, I saw a parade from a Los Angeles apartment-house balcony that I didn't understand because I was a little girl. There were no decorated floats, no bands, no horses and riders, no flags, and no laughter or joy. It was a silent parade made up of trucks and cars, each piled high with boxes, bundles, and furniture. Men, women, and children walked behind the heavily laden vehicles. Many carried suitcases, and some of the women carried their babies. Older children clutched the hands of younger ones. Everyone wore shipping tags tied to their buttonholes. The tags flapped and fluttered in the breeze as the people walked past.

It was an orderly, quiet, sad parade. The balcony observers were silent, also. The people below were their neighbors and friends. Some had tears in their eyes.

I asked my mother, "Where are they going?" "To an internment camp," she replied. "What's an internment camp?" "Never mind, you're too young to understand."

It was many years later that I actually learned about Executive Order 9066 and what had happened that day in front of the Vanderbilt Apartments in Los Angeles, California.

ABOUT THE QUILT

Once Donna decided to make a quilt about what she had seen, she conducted research and thought about the images she would use. Internment articles in magazines at her local library had been torn out. It was necessary to get copies from the Library of Congress in Washington, D.C., but Donna and a friendly librarian persevered.

In "Exodus: April 1942" the silhouetted family, shipping labels attached, stand out against a pieced background made from the Whirlwind block. Donna used a swirling, abstract decorator print and further enhanced the image with a design for machine-quilted swirls. She selected Whirlwind to symbolize motion, but also the confusion and turbulence caused by the gossip and rumors that had everyone frightened. I also see the desert winds the families found at the end of their journeys. Others have seen the "winds of war."

For her borders, Donna used more silhouettes, Flying Geese blocks, and an abstract "fence" print. Japanese *yukata* fabrics, used in piecing Flying Geese blocks, symbolized the Japanese-American families; khaki prints represented the United States Army soldiers who accompanied and guarded the families at the camps.

Donna recalled a part of her own childhood that needed to be shared with her grandchildren. She not only wrote about her memories in a memory book, she made a quilt to graphically illustrate her story.

Special Points
- Embellished with tags
- Pieced background
- Theme blocks
- Decorator fabrics
- Ethnic Japanese fabric

Quilt Blocks

Flying Geese   Whirlwind

HISTORY AS LIVED BY A PARTICIPANT:

"Letting Go" by Naoko Anne Ito

Locally my *Nisei* (second-generation Japanese American) friends were involved in making the quilt "Threads of Remembrance" for the Oakland Museum show "Strength and Diversity: Japanese American Women 1885 to 1990." I kept urging Anne to make her own quilt featuring the internment of Japanese Americans, but she reminded me that the internment had been a sad time in her life, and she didn't want to dwell on it. Stubbornly, I replied there had to have been five minutes of happiness she could tell about.

When Anne joined a story quilt class, much to my amazement she announced, "Well, I have my camp story!"

Photo 7-6.
Letting Go.
Naoko Anne Ito.
See also
Color Plate 30.

ANNE'S STORY

During World War II, because of my Japanese ancestry, we were incarcerated in the Relocation Camp in Heart Mountain, Wyoming. We could only take what we could carry, which meant no pets. One day in camp, my brother and I found a small bird and captured it and had Father make a cage for it. We noticed that the mother bird, fighting her fear of humans, brought her baby bird a worm each day for one week. Since we could no longer stand separating the mother and baby, we let our pet go. I was fifteen years old.

ABOUT THE QUILT

Once "Letting Go" had come to her, Anne was ready to begin. For the camp housing, she symbolically used dark antique Japanese mens' clothing purchased at a flea market in Japan. The ever-present tower and mountains would be in the background. For the pieced sky and pieced foreground she decided to use two blocks: Birds in the Air and Flying Bird, respectively.

The foreground was hardest to portray. In her box of Japanese fabrics, I discovered two colorways of a wonderful "rock" fabric and suggested using them. I had seen Ansel Adam's striking photographs of Camp Manzanar in California which showed rocks as part of the terrain. Though Anne said there weren't rocks like those at Heart Mountain, the rock fabric could be symbolic of the desolate place they were taken, of the hard times they endured. (Coloring the Flying Bird blocks to create a neutralized pieced foreground is discussed on page 73.)

Anne saved the center of her quilt for the figures of herself and her brother. Their arms are outstretched as they bid farewell to their pet. Anne's story is true, but it is also a metaphor of her own imprisoned teen years.

Special Points
- Ethnic Japanese fabric
- Pieced sky
- Hand-dyed fabrics
- Pieced foreground
- Theme blocks
- Theme fabrics
- Theme back

Quilt Blocks

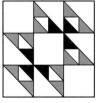

Birds in the Air   Flying Bird

Photo 7-7. *Letting Go.* **(detail: sky pieced with three sizes of Birds in the Air block).**

MAN-MADE DISASTERS:

"Minor Inconveniences"
by Bonnie Bucknam Holmstrand

Sometimes we start out on a quilting project with certain thoughts in mind, but by the time the project is finished, we end up with a different interpretation of our finished results. This happened with Bonnie's quilt.

Photo 7-8. *Minor Inconveniences.* **Bonnie Bucknam Holmstrand. Photo by G. Craig Freas. See also Color Plate 31.**

BONNIE'S STORY

I began a quilt when Judy Hopkins put out the call for quilts for her new Bow Tie book, Fit to Be Tied. *When the top was completed, I took it to work to share. My job involves time spent on the Valdez oil spill litigation, and when my co-workers saw the quilt, they immediately insisted I had created an oil spill quilt! Here are some of their comments:*

"It looks like an aerial oil tracking map: the white represents lightly oiled; red, moderately oiled; black, heavily oiled."

"Cars are piled up waiting for gas because of the oil shortages caused by the spill."

"The airplane fabric shows the aerial overflights."

"The sea shell and vegetation fabric represent the organisms that made the oil in the first place."

"Fish are swimming through black oiled water. One fabric shows dead birds."

"There are animal tracks in the oil and oil splatters everywhere."

"The white polka-dot on black in the border looks like a chemical dispersants test."

Because of the media attention to the oil spill and their personal involvement, my audience had new eyes to see my work. I tried to insist that quilting was how I took my mind off my work, but my co-workers prevailed. "We don't care what you think you did; you made an oil spill quilt!" I gave up. As I thought about it, I had come up with the idea for the quilt after the spill had taken place. Now the Bow Ties came to represent huge corporations; the Pinwheels, corporate chaos. I decided I might as well give the quilt the identity it was seeking. The title, "Minor Inconveniences," was derived from a news quote of an oil company official who apologized for "any inconvenience" the biggest oil spill in the nation's history might have caused the people of Alaska.

ABOUT THE QUILT

Bonnie's top is basically abstract, even though it is pieced from two traditional blocks. She first placed the two blocks randomly in a nonspecific repeat pattern in the center section of the quilt. She then colored the blocks in a nontraditional way by also placing the printed fabrics in a random rather than expected way in each block.

Bonnie has used a wide selection of fabrics that can be tied to the oil spill theme. For example, cars and planes use oil products. (Upon close observation, I found the car and airplane fabrics I used in my earthquake quilt.) She also represented the organic matter which formed the oil. As a result of the spill, much plant and animal life was killed. The borders containing plant and fish prints are particularly telling and graphic. (The drawing for her quilting design is shown in Figure 8-27.)

Special Points
• Theme blocks
• Theme fabrics

Quilt Blocks

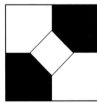
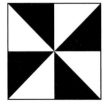

Bow Tie   Pinwheel

PROMOTING WORTHY CAUSES:

"Ivory Is for Elephants"
by Barbara Dallas

Times change. Today we speak of environmental issues we didn't even think about in the not-so-distant past. Barbara chose one such issue.

Photo 7-9. *Ivory Is for Elephants*. Barbara Dallas. See also Color Plate 32.

Photo 7-10. *Ivory Is for Elephants* (detail).

BARBARA'S STORY

The idea for this project came while watching a documentary on public television called "Ivory Wars." At one stage in the program, the brutal slaughter of an elephant was depicted. In this scene, the elephant's face was shorn off with a chain saw to liberate its tusks from its body. I found this image profoundly disturbing and one which lingered on in my mind's eye for quite some time. It was this image which prompted me to make this quilt as my personal statement against the slaughter of such majestic creatures.

I visited the local public library to read up on the ivory and elephants issue. To my surprise, I found elephant behavior is very much like human behavior: they are willing to go to great lengths to protect their offspring, and they have very loving and nurturing relationships with them.

Humans were slaughtering and decimating these noble beasts so their ivory could be sold to other people who wanted to adorn themselves and their homes with baubles and trinkets. Idealistically, I would like to believe that if there is no longer a consumer market for ivory products, then this senseless massacre of the African elephant population will end. If seeing my quilt will cause even one person to think twice before purchasing ivory, then it will have been more than worth the time and effort it took to complete this project

ABOUT THE QUILT

Barbara used Versatex textile paints, indelible ink pens, and single strands of DMC embroidery floss to draw her images. She began with a majestic elephant head which she encircled in a ring of pieced jungle fabrics. Rather than using the entire circle, she cropped one side for a more interesting composition. Groupings of elephants appear in two border areas. For the third border area, Barbara has chosen to show an assortment of ivory items, from piano keys to Japanese netsukes, cascading into a packing box labeled with an international red "forbidden" symbol.

As Barbara worked on her quilt, she read newspaper reports of decreased ivory sales in the United States as the result of a federal importation ban in 1989. Potential purchasers weren't even interested in stocks on hand. Even though the United States accounted for only ten to fifteen percent of the ivory purchased, times were changing.

Barbara Dallas, a quilter like countless others in the United States and around the world, decided to speak out for the first time on a social issue that troubled her. In the process, she didn't concern herself with whether or not her quilt was "pretty." She learned some surprising things and enriched her own life.

Special Points
• Textile paints
• Permanent marking pens
• Embroidery
• Reverse appliqué words

8. Design

Is starting to design your quilt one of the hardest parts of making it for you? It is for many other quilters, too. Even students who come to a story quilt class knowing their topic are often overwhelmed with the details they think need to be included, if the story is to be told.

FINDING A FOCUS FOR YOUR DESIGN

Before beginning to design your quilt, review your subject, and see what you have on hand in your file folder. Go over your story idea, and add things you may have remembered since you first thought of it. Details have a way of resurfacing and coming back to us. If it's been awhile since you've gone over the material, take time to reacquaint yourself with what you've collected. Your folder will probably contain quite an assortment:

- written notes
- appropriate quilt block names and designs
- photographs
- sketches for possible layouts
- pictures from newspapers and magazines
- advertising brochures and mailers
- memorabilia (postcards, flyers, brochures)

Spread out the contents of your folder and sort them into appropriate piles. You will begin to see that some of your materials are great; others, not as great anymore. The editing process can help you zero in on your ideas. Remember, you want to come up with a project of manageable size. Think in terms of creating a quilt snapshot, not *War and Peace*.

DEVISING A DESIGN FORMAT

There are many ways to create a design for your story quilt. Quilters vary widely in the process they use to produce their designs. Some are comfortable with grabbing a piece of fabric and going directly to their design wall with it. At the other extreme are those who spend days sketching before they cut into their fabric. It is possible to be somewhere in between, of course. You may even know what part of your quilt will look like, but not have a clue what will happen after that. It can all work.

Try using a different method of quilt design, even though it may make you uncomfortable. Doing things differently can help you stretch and grow, and it will give you an alternate way of problem-solving for future designs if your normal procedure doesn't work for you. As quilters, we often settle on an easy, comfortable solution, and jump into the "making" too soon. Our designs might be better, and benefit greatly, if we spent more time on them.

I ask story class participants to develop three design compositions for their quilt before they begin construction. In a one-day class, things are a bit hurried and we make only a beginning on the designs. However, at the end of a two-day class when the three designs are shared, it's particularly interesting to see the results and the progress each student has made during the day of "forced" design time. I have included the sketch work that was a part of creating some of the quilts in this book to illustrate the twists and turns the process can take.

USING IMAGES

Maybe you already have a specific image in your mind for a story quilt. There are a number of ways to transfer your mental image to fabric.

You can begin by drawing a picture of your story. In fact, this obvious solution usually emerges first when students have to come up with three ways of presenting their story. (Emma Allebes had her grandchildren make drawings to use in the upper portion of her quilt instead.) I have included three of the five preliminary sketches B. J. Welden did for "Emma's Eggs." (See Figures 8-1, 8-2, and 8-3.) Four of her sketches were pictorial, and one had a slightly more abstract format.

If you draw a "good" picture, you will need to enlarge it. Use the standard grid method of enlarging. The original is gridded into squares and then a larger paper is also gridded with larger squares. Rather than trying to copy the whole drawing, concentrate on one section at a time. If an area is too complicated, it can also be further subdivided. (See the example in Figure 8-4.) If your drawing is small, use the enlarging feature on a copy machine to make it larger.

**Figure 8-1.
Sketch #1.
B. J. Welden.**

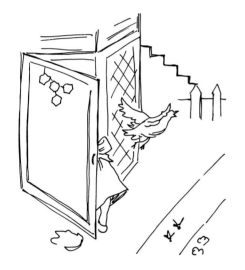

**Figure 8-2.
Sketch #2.
B. J. Welden.**

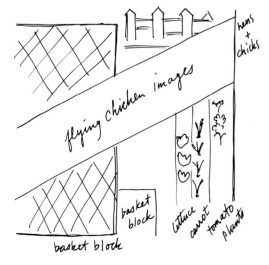

**Figure 8-3.
Sketch #3.
B. J. Welden.**

**Figure 8-4.
Grid method of
enlargement.**

Your drawing can also be projected to the desired size onto butcher paper, taped to a wall, using an opaque projector. (These handy devices are often advertised in quilt magazines, or they can be purchased through art supply stores. Sometimes schools or libraries make them available to use on site.) In this way you end up with a full-size cartoon from which individual templates can be made.

It is also possible to take a slide of your picture and project the image on the wall with a slide projector to make a full-size cartoon. If you don't own a slide projector, local camera shops usually rent them.

You could also work directly from a slide you have taken. (If you are worried about fading it, a duplicate can be made by a photo lab. The lab can make slides from regular photographs, too.) Another possibility is to copy and enlarge your slides or photos on a copy machine. Then make a cartoon, using the grid or opaque projection methods.

If you absolutely can't draw, you might enjoy trying paper cutting. For some reason, paper cutting shuts off the voice in your left brain that likes to tell you that you can't draw. Once you fool yourself, it's amazing what can happen. Many students who are adamant about their lack of artistic ability do quite well with this technique.

As you cut, keep in mind that paper is cheap. If the first try doesn't produce the desired results, try again, and again. Tossing aside a misfire or crumbling it up doesn't seem to have the negative imprint of failure that using an eraser does. You can paper cut from your imagination or paper cut while looking at real objects and pictures. Both ways work.

The Mercy girls that float in the sky of "Farewell to Mercy" were paper cut. (See Photo 8-1.) You have probably made paper dolls in this manner at one time or another. Next time you decide you can't draw, try this method.

Another way to come up with an image is to get warmed up by doing a collage with colored pictures from magazines. I made a collage of my childhood trip to California in an art class. Later, when I wanted to treat my

Photo 8-1. *Farewell to Mercy* **(detail: paper-cut Mercy girls). Mary Mashuta.**

Photo 8-2. Trip to California collage. Mary Mashuta, Dorr Bothwell collage class, Mendocino Art Center, 1986.

quilt image in a more abstract way, I remembered the collage. (See Photo 8-2.)

While you're working with your drawing or picture, think about its composition. Is it possible to make it better by making changes? Would the image be more interesting if it were cropped, if some of it was cut off? It may not be necessary to see the whole scene. A tighter, closer image may be more appealing.

What would happen if the literal image is fractured, or broken apart, into its individual parts? Perhaps the parts which make up the whole can be used as elements by themselves in the overall composition. In the end, the whole, complete image might not even be a part of the quilt: the elements of which it is comprised may do just as well. Take as an example the process used by Bonnie Holmstrand when she designed "One Arm Bandit." She began by sketching actual shirts she had brought to class, concentrating on the individual shirt parts; she experimented with how they could be drawn in a repeat format (Figure 8-5). Then she drew sketches for four possible quilt designs using the shirt elements; a fifth was drawn several months later before she began actual construction (Figures 8-6 through 8-10).

You can also add photographs as an embellishment to a story quilt, rather than using them as the source of the main design image. Try to get beyond merely connecting a series of photograph blocks with sashing and setting them into a traditional grid. More interesting design possibilities exist.

You can attach photographs directly to the surface of a wallhanging quilt, but most often quilters transfer their photographs to fabric before incorporating them into their quilts. Leslie Hatch-Wong used three colored prints in "Someday May They All Be Free." She enlarged them on a color copier and then sent the copies off to be transferred to beige fabric. Using beige rather than white fabric helped blend the transfers more smoothly into her rust and beige monochromatic color scheme. (See Photo 4-4.)

For "Westward Ho!" I used commercially transferred photos on fabric as part of the appliquéd and pieced border designs. For three borders, the photograph was incorporated into similar architectural motifs: southwestern-

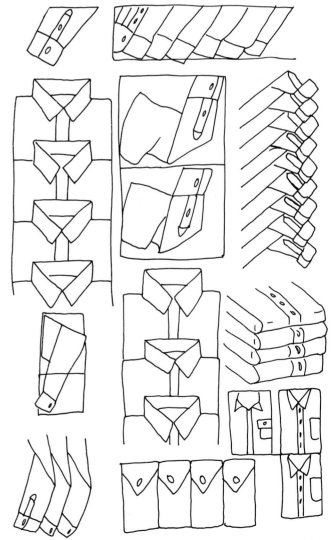

Figure 8-5. Preliminary sketches. Bonnie Bucknam Holmstrand.

Figure 8-6. Sketch: Version #1. Bonnie Bucknam Holmstrand.

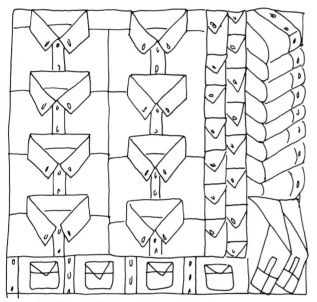

Figure 8-7. Sketch: Version #2. Bonnie Bucknam Holmstrand.

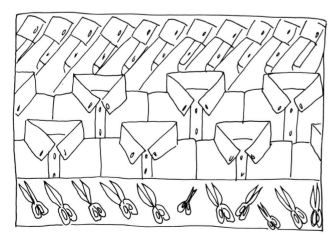

Figure 8-8. Sketch: Version #3. Bonnie Bucknam Holmstrand.

Figure 8-9. Sketch: Version #4. Bonnie Bucknam Holmstrand.

Figure 8-10. Sketch: Version #5. Bonnie Bucknam Holmstrand.

feeling shrines or niches (Photo 8-3). The fourth photo was placed in a sunburst motif in the top border. I began with a black-and-white photograph. After it was transferred to fabric, I ended up with four monotones: mulberry, ocher, blue, and black. Monotones are considerably cheaper than color pictures and can be made from either black-and-white or color prints. You can plan your overall color scheme around the colors available.

In "Coming to Terms" I "hid" military photos in my swirling jungle. I used both black and green monotones to blend into the color scheme. To make the photos less noticeable, the light background behind each figure was cut away and then the silhouettes were hand appliquéd in place (Photo 7-2).

To give equal time to the Peace Movement in "Coming to Terms," I added photos to the quilt back as well as the front. Again I used black and green monotones. To make the "peace rally" photo more interesting design-wise, I cropped the rectangular picture, angling the top and bottom edges. To reduce the areas of light value, I machine stitched each in place with four rows of dark stitching and added a fabric "fragment." The pictures become design elements, not just afterthoughts (Photo 7-4).

Consider incorporating photos in the design of the quilt back, if they don't seem appropriate for the front. For example, for the back of "Capezio Shoe-fly," I pieced four Shoo-fly blocks. Photos on fabric were substituted for the fabric in the center squares of each block. This is a good way to add documentation to your quilt. (See Photos 2-12 and 8-4.)

A photograph of my mother appears on the back of "Hanky for the Teacher." (See both the Dedication page

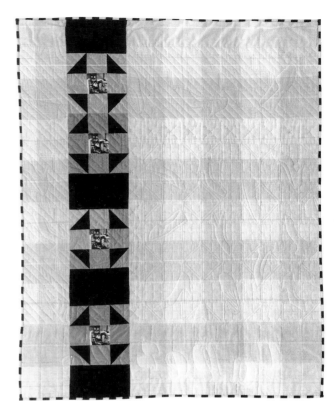

Photo 8-4. *Capezio Shoe-fly* (back). Mary Mashuta.

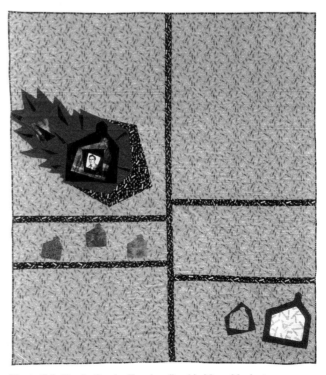

Photo 8-5. *Hanky for the Teacher* (back). Mary Mashuta.

Photo 8-3. *Westward Ho!* (detail: photo niche). Mary Mashuta.

and Photo 8-5.) To make the back theme-appropriate, I used two color versions of a crayon print with school-house cutouts. The transferred photo is included in a schoolhouse collage which zooms across the sky just like Dorothy did in the "Wizard of Oz."

Remember, the quality of the transfer image is never as good as your original, though often that's acceptable. The pictures that make the best transfers have good value contrast. Check this on a copy machine. If everything muddies together, it's a good indication of what will happen in the transfer.

Most often the piece of fabric is stiffer after the picture is applied. Consider this when incorporating the transfer into your design.

Using mail-away processes takes time. (I usually want my pictures the day before yesterday.) Express Mail, Federal Express, or similar services can help to speed up things.

If you are reluctant to part with your photographs or would like to do some experimenting, you may be interested in *Fabric Photos* by Marjorie Croner.

If you have the original photo negatives of your pictures, consider using transfer fabric from Blue-Printables. You are limited to the size of your negative and to the color blue. The method can also be used to make silhouettes of found objects to incorporate in your design.

If the process of image transfer intrigues you and you'd like to experiment a little, try the transfer gel products called By Jupiter!®, Picture This™, or Stitchless Fabric Glue and Transfer Medium. They can be used with magazine photographs and/or copy machine images of pictures. (Addresses for these products are given in the Appendix.)

BUILDING THE QUILT AROUND QUILT BLOCKS

Checking quilt magazines and quilt compendiums for possible blocks is one of the easiest parts of developing a quilt design.

Most people come up with a number of appropriate blocks for their story quilt (usually more than they can use). Celia LoPinto used seven blocks in "The Hurricane of 1938" and Kathy Dimond used seven in "Sierra Getaway," but in most cases it will be necessary to narrow the choice of blocks to one or two. Look over your collection and answer these questions for each block:

- Do I like the appearance of the block?
- Would I enjoy drafting and piecing it?
- If it is too complicated to draft, or if there are too many pieces, can I find a simpler version?
- What does the block look like when repeated?

When you have selected your block or blocks, what comes next? Quilt blocks can be used in a variety of ways in designing a story quilt. One of the most popular traditional quilts is one that simply repeats a block over and over. Usually the blocks are set off with sashing or alternate plain blocks. Sometimes each block is the same color and fabric; other times blocks are made from scraps. This design format can always be used for a story quilt, but there are other possibilities you may enjoy exploring.

For example, contortion, or distortion, can be used to change the appearance of the basic block. This has been particularly popular among traditional quilters who want their work to look more contemporary. In a very simple example of contortion, I broke up the garment design area of "Gaijin." My basic block was a square divided into two equal triangles. Because the block was so simple, I changed the size of rows since I couldn't break up the grid of the basic block (Figure 8-11).

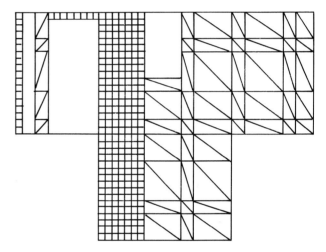

Figure 8-11. Sketch: *Gaijin.* Mary Mashuta.

To break up more complicated blocks, divide the block into its basic units and rows. Then, rather than drawing all sections of the basic block grid the same size, the height and/or width of rows can be changed. After the basic grid is altered, the individual units are drawn in the new grid.

Using the Shoo-fly block, let's look at some preliminary drawings for "Capezio Shoe-fly" as an example of contorting the grid. Figure 8-12 shows the standard nine-patch block. Figures 8-13 and 8-14 show two possible designs achieved by contorting the grid and then filling in the blocks. This was only a beginning: other options would result from changes in the basic grid.

Quilters have been interested in designing quilts in which backgrounds were seen through grids. The challenge of creating the optical illusion is intriguing. Some traditional blocks can create wonderful grids when a number are pieced and joined. I first used one in "Hanky for the

Figure 8-12.
Shoo-fly block.

Figure 8-13.
Sketch: contorted grid A
using Shoo-fly block.
Mary Mashuta.

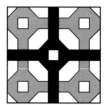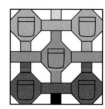

Figure 8-15.
Tile Puzzle
block changed
to Hanky
Puzzle block.

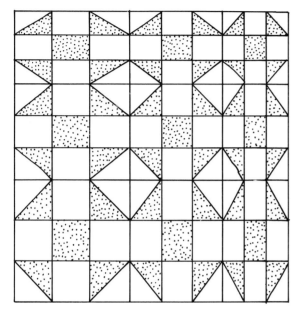

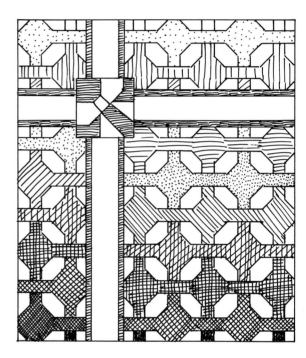

Figure 8-16. Sketch: *Hanky for the Teacher* using Tile Puzzle block. **Mary Mashuta.**

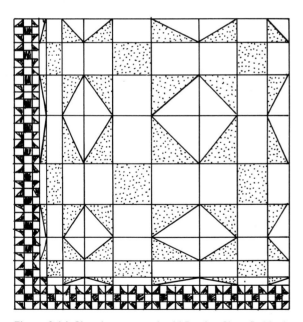

Figure 8-14. Sketch: contorted grid B using Shoo-fly block. Mary Mashuta.

Teacher." I changed Tile Puzzle to Hanky Puzzle by adding a pocket (Figure 8-15).The block allowed me to have an interlocking foreground grid and background negative space in which I could use a color flow. (See my sketch for the quilt in Figure 8-16.)

When I later designed "Coming to Terms," I drew a sketch which would give me areas in which to display my jungle and patriotic fabrics (Figure 8-17). Then I discovered another puzzle-type pattern to use instead. Patriot's Quilt had a larger negative space than Tile Puzzle. I decided to customize the basic block by breaking it into more pieces (so I could use a greater variety of fabric) and to rename it Vietnam Patriot's block. (See both blocks in Figure 8-18.) Now look at Photo 8-6 to see the grid done in fabric. A lot of red was used in piecing the grid; cooler greens appear in the background areas. Red comes forward because it is warm; green recedes because it is cool. Many of the greens were also grayed and murky which helped even more to keep them in the optical background. (See also Color Plate 28.)

Bev Karau drew two preliminary drawings for her quilt "Incident at Harris Ranch" using the Cotton Reels and Aircraft blocks (Figures 8-19 and 8-20). Bev combined elements from both sketches for her actual quilt. Photo 5-5 shows a detail of the quilt with the field pieced in perspective. Doing the cotton field in perspective was a new

Figure 8-17. Sketch: *Coming to Terms.* Mary Mashuta.

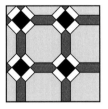 

Figure 8-18. Patriot's Quilt block expanded to Vietnam Patriot's Quilt block.

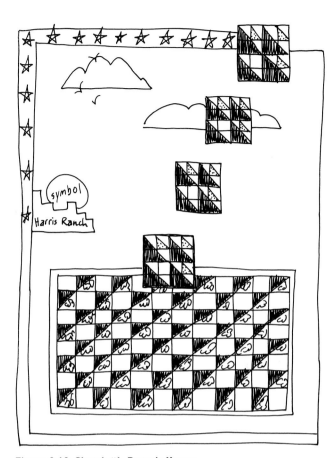

Figure 8-19. Sketch #1. Beverly Karau.

Photo 8-6. *Coming to Terms* (detail: side 1 grid). Mary Mashuta.

Figure 8-20. Sketch #2: blocks drawn in perspective. Beverly Karau.

experience for Bev. She consulted Katie Pasquini's book *3 Dimensional Design* and decided to try two-point perspective. Since each piece was a different size, accuracy was really important if it was all going to fit together when the quilt was assembled. Also note Bev has altered the final downed Aircraft block by distorting the normally square extended four-patch block.

Quilt Blocks as Borders

Repeat blocks are often used to create borders around the central panel of a quilt. There are no rules saying you have to limit yourself to one-block borders or that all your borders have to be made from the same size blocks. Lighten up your thinking about borders and see what happens.

A word of caution, however. Stay away from borders that are mere collections of all the blocks you have found relating to your theme. They are likely to take on the appearance of a sampler. The viewer spends too much time decoding the blocks, and the overall effect is choppy: the eye makes too many stops as it reads the quilt.

Karren Elsbernd created mixed technique borders for "February 10th" using hearts, eyelet, and ribbon blocks (Photo 2-7). Jeanie Smith had two pieced Delectable Mountains borders and two appliquéd fish borders in "Lucy Flagbody Goes Fishing" (Photo 4-8). Donna Holt

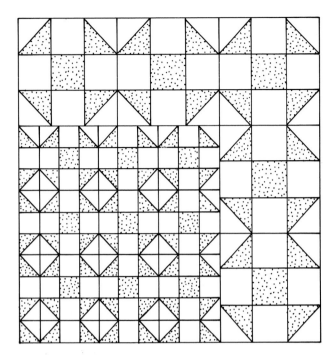

Figure 8-21. Sketch #1: 15" Shoo-fly blocks plus 9" Shoo-fly blocks. Mary Mashuta.

Figure 8-22. Sketch: *Capezio Shoe-fly*. Mary Mashuta.

Photo 8-7. *Capezio Shoe-fly*. Mary Mashuta.

used Flying Geese for two borders in "Exodus: April 1942," and then switched to plaid fabric for the third border and appliquéd silhouettes for the fourth (Photo 7-5).

Individual borders may be both pieced and appliquéd as in "Farewell to Mercy" (Photo 4-10). Remember, however, I was going for chaos and frenzy. In a much simpler combination border, Celia LoPinto reinforced the theme of "The Devastating Storm of 1938" by using two Ocean Waves blocks to intersect the vertical two-fabric borders (Photo 2-13). Several stray, contrasting triangles float away from the tightly pieced transitional blocks. This clever device provides a pleasing diversion in the successful transition between the upper and lower fabrics.

Quilt Blocks as Background

Consider using a repeated pieced block as the background negative space of your quilt. It can be much more interesting than using a solid piece of fabric, but it does take more work. Select your colors carefully so they will remain in the background optically. The quilters who used this design device achieved subtle color effects using low value contrasts and grayed colors.

If you have never thought of using a pieced background, you might enjoy how I developed one for "Capezio Shoe-fly" using the Shoo-fly block. I knew I wanted to scatter realistic shoes across some kind of pieced background. After trying contorted grids, I wondered what would happen if I tried using different-sized blocks together? In Figure 8-21, I began with five 15" blocks arranged in an upside down "L" configuration. I then tried to inset a set of smaller 9" blocks to fill in the square area, but discovered I had partial blocks left over. If I didn't resort to higher math to redraft the block, I would have to use a 3" inset. I had also begun to worry about how the two sets of blocks would look butting against each other. How about a line of 3" contrasting Shoo-Fly blocks to fill in the leftover space? Compare my final drawing (Figure 8-22) with the completed quilt seen in black and white (Photo 8-7). Note the subtle value contrast in the 15" and 9" blocks. The background has variety—it's not flat and dull. Now look at Color Plate 5. The background has life, but it doesn't upstage the shoes, the real stars of the piece.

Anne Ito pieced two portions of her quilt "Letting Go" with repeated blocks. The Birds in the Air block was pieced for the sky, but she broke up the area by combining an assortment of 9", 6", and 3" blocks. The variety in value and pattern Anne achieved by combining hand-dyed fabric from Debra Lunn with other "sky" fabrics from her collection is especially clear in Photo 7-7. Now compare with Color Plate 30 to see how the closeness of hue keeps the sky as background.

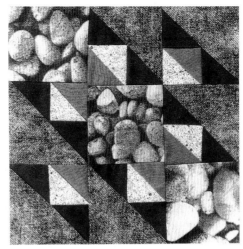

Photo 8-8. Flying Bird block. Naoko Anne Ito.

Photo 8-9. *Letting Go* (detail: foreground). Naoko Anne Ito.

Anne had some problems with the Flying Bird blocks she used in the foreground. Photo 8-8 shows an early version of the block, pieced with dark, medium, and light value contrast. Anne had learned her basic quilting lessons too well. There is too much contrast for a series of these blocks to read as background because it's too easy to see the individual units. The eye doesn't flow over the surface. Compare this block with Anne's improved blocks in the final version (Photo 8-9). What a difference narrowing the value range makes when the darker values are removed.

George Taylor also wanted to play with background color, so he created George's Schoolhouse from the block Ohio Schoolhouse (Figure 8-23) and used it for the background of "Little Redheaded Girl." He's a draftsman, so it was easy for him to fiddle with the block enough to make it interlock in stacking rows. Compare his drawing (Figure 8-24) with the center portion of the quilt (Photo 8-10).

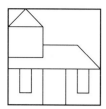

Figure 8-23. Ohio Schoolhouse block.

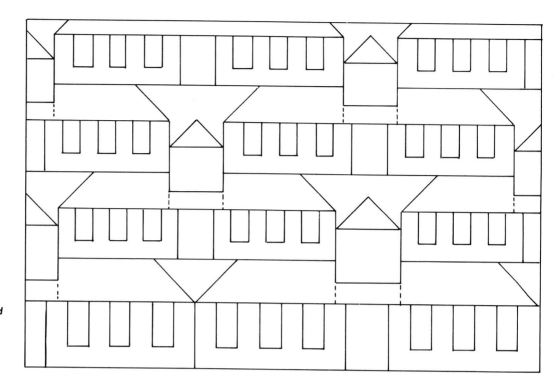

Figure 8-24. Sketch: *Little Redheaded Girl.* **George Taylor.**

Photo 8-10. *Little Redheaded Girl* (detail: center panel). **George Taylor.**

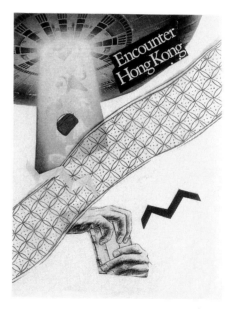

Photo 8-11. Collage for *Hong Kong Blues.* **Kay Sakanashi.**

Kay Sakanashi planned "Hong Kong Blues" and its pieced background following another procedure. First she made a collage (Photo 8-11) on notebook paper, using magazine pictures and Japanese wrapping paper, to get a general idea of what her design would look like. After selecting the block Crosses and Losses, she drew it in a repeat block format (Figure 8-25). The sketch proved to be an unsatisfactory solution, however, because she had decided to do a value study from dark to light, and she couldn't show the necessary progression with pencil. Kay had done fabric glued mock-ups in my color class so she decided to try one here. She then used the mock-up (Photo 8-12) as a guide to piece the actual top.

Figure 8-25. Sketch: Repeated Crosses and Losses blocks. Kay Sakanashi.
▼

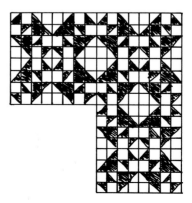

Photo 8-12. Glued mock-up for *Hong Kong Blues*. Kay Sakanashi.

Photo 8-13. *Capezio Shoe-fly* (detail: front side quilt top). Mary Mashuta. Photo by Mary Mashuta.

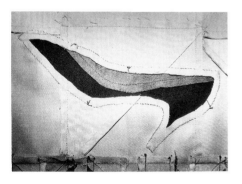

Photo 8-14. *Capezio Shoe-fly* (detail: back side quilt top). Mary Mashuta. Photo by Mary Mashuta.

After you have pieced a background, you may want to add appliqué motifs to it. When your stitching is complete, cut out the excess fabric on the back side to reduce bulk before the top is quilted. This step also eliminates, or reduces, shadowing through by a printed or dark colored fabric. Photos 8-13 and 8-14 show the front and back side of a hand appliquéd shoe that has been properly trimmed. (This step will not be possible if you have used fusibles with machine appliqué.)

DESIGNING WITHOUT QUILT BLOCKS

Although many story quilts are built around "theme" quilt blocks, it isn't necessary to do this to have a quilt qualify as a story quilt. However, it is wonderful when the individual parts of the quilt can reinforce the theme or add design interest to the total composition.

For example, if you want to float objects on a background but don't want to do a complicated pieced one of blocks, try something simpler. Barbara Dallas divided the background of "Fritz's Dimond Roller Rink" into four random sections, and then used a variety of small-scale neutral plaids to piece them (Photo 3-9).

It's also possible to create borders that enhance your story without using traditional pieced blocks. Lynn Brown used Aztec motifs found in old documents. "Towers," fish, and ray motifs were used for inner and outer borders for her quilt "I Just Want To Make Red Shoes." She further reinforced her theme by using culturally appropriate colors (Photo 4-11).

The mixed technique theme borders for my "Westward Ho!" were created to enhance four appliqué blocks that contained my trip photos. In Photo 8-15 the borders have been separated. They are similar, but each is a little differ-

Karren Elsbernd also decided to do a value study as she pieced the background of "February 10th" in a disappearing pattern of blocks. She used the Cake Stand block. (Photo 2-7). In other quilts, Donna Holt used a repeated Whirlwind block behind her silhouettes in "Exodus: April 1942" (Photo 7-5). The piecing design was simple—she let her swirling, abstract fabric do the work. B. J. Welden used two blocks in "Emma's Eggs": Hen and Chickens in the foreground, Birds in the Air in the sky (Photo 3-7). Mabry Benson used Milky Way to create a nighttime sky in "Smokey the Cat: Rescue at Midnight" (Photo 3-13).

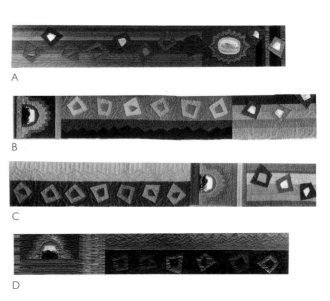

Photo 8-15. *Westward Ho!* (borders separated). Mary Mashuta.

ent from the others. The majority of the work was appliquéd, but machine strip piecing was also a design element in three of the contiguous borders as they formed the top of the quilt. The borders were designed spontaneously as I went along, beginning with the lower one and ending with the top. This last border was the hardest to create because I wanted it to be lighter in feeling since it was at the top, and I also had to use it to tie the other three together.

Judy Sogn created borders to support the central scene in "Feasts and Facets: Memories of Portugal." Though dissimilar in appearance, they all relate to her theme. This adds variety to the quilt. The borders have been separated in Photo 8-16. Note that they aren't all

Photo 8-17. *Fritz's Dimond Roller Rink* **(details: border corners). Barbara Dallas.**

the same width, and opposite ones don't match in size: two are 5" wide, one is 6", and one is 8½". The lower border reaches from one side of the quilt to the other and adds compositional weight and stability to the bottom of the quilt. There's no rule that says all the borders must be the same width—you may just have been assuming it exists!

Determining the size of borders like these is often intuitive, and the exact measurements are arrived at by experimenting a little. Graph paper is helpful for quick sketches. Although the size of any border can theoretically be altered, pieced borders are usually adjusted by adding or subtracting a unit or by changing the block size. Appliqué is easier to fiddle with since the background can be adjusted slightly or the images made a little smaller or larger.

Barbara Dallas created a lovely Art Deco border for her quilt "Fritz's Dimond Roller Rink." She was especially clever in doing her color change as she went around two of the corners. (See details of the corners in Photo 8-17.)

USING WORDS ON QUILTS

Some people like the graphic quality that words on quilts impart or the meaning they add; others feel these visual "hints" shouldn't be there to clutter up the viewer's interpretation of the piece. If you decide to use words on your

A

B

C

D

Photo 8-16. *Feasts and Facets: Memories of Portugal* **(borders separated). Judy Sogn.**

Photo 8-18. *Quake of '89* **(back detail: computerized machine stitching). Mary Mashuta.**

Photo 8-19. *Farewell to Mercy* **(detail: waste canvas embroidery). Mary Mashuta.**

Photo 8-20. *Farewell to Mercy* (detail: light color reverse appliquéd letters). Mary Mashuta.

Photo 8-21. *Farewell to Mercy* (detail: dark color reverse appliquéd letters). Mary Mashuta.

Photo 8-22. *Farewell to Mercy* (detail: close-up of reverse appliquéd letter that has been quilted). Mary Mashuta.

carefully. Photo 8-20 shows a light letter reverse appliquéd into a dark background. There will be no surprises here. When I picked the background stripe fabric in Photo 8-21, however, I forgot the letter's seam allowance would shadow through in the white areas of the stripe. I finally overcame the problem by quilting around the letter in the striped background with blue-green thread that matched the letter color. This seemed to blur the shadow.

Photo 8-22 shows how to outline a reverse appliquéd letter with quilting stitches. A second line of quilting can also be added in the background fabric ¼" away from the background edge.

CREATING QUILT BACKS

Quilt designing used to be over when the front was designed and executed. Not so anymore. We can add to what is happening on the front by continuing on in some fashion on the back. It entails more work than a plain back, but it can be lots of fun.

Photo 8-23. *Fritz's Dimond Roller Rink* (detail: back fabric). Barbara Dallas.

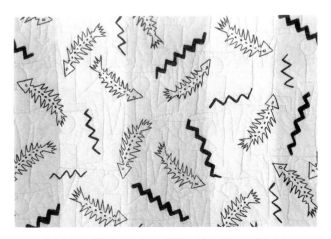

Photo 8-24. *Lucy Flagbody Goes Fishing* (detail: back fabric). Jeanie Smith.

quilt, there are a number of ways to incorporate verbiage beyond designing a quilt label. On the back of "Quake of '89," I used my computerized Bernina to add statistics about the earthquake (Photo 8-18). This feature is also great for quilt labels.

For "Farewell to Mercy," I used waste, or destruct, canvas and DMC Perle cotton thread to cross-stitch part of a line from my Mercy story (Photo 8-19). Once again, this technique could be used to make a quilt label.

Part of my designs for "Farewell to Mercy" and "Capezio Shoe-fly" were large graphic words done in reverse appliqué. I find this technique easier than regular appliqué for doing objects like letters which have many curves. When doing reverse appliqué, select your fabrics

Photo 8-25.
Gaijin (back).
Mary Mashuta.

The easiest way to create a story back is to find an appropriate theme fabric. Keep this in mind as you collect your fabrics. I used crayon prints for "Farewell to Mercy" and "Hanky for the Teacher." When Barbara Dallas came across a roller-skating fabric, she knew she would use it someday. And since she wanted to use appliqué on the front of "Fritz's Dimond Roller Rink," the roller skating print was happily relegated to the quilt back (Photo 8-23). Jeanie Smith bought a fish fabric for "Lucy Flagbody Goes Fishing" (Photo 8-24), and Judy Sogn found a hill-town scene for "Feasts and Facets: Memories of Portugal" (Photo 6-5). This must have been a generic hill-town fabric because Lynn Brown also used it for part of the back of "I Just Want to Make Red Shoes." Lynn said it reminded her of Mexico!

To personalize quilt backs, blocks can be repeated from the front as additional theme reinforcement. Karren Elsbernd added a checkerboard heart block and a Valentine label to the back of "February 10th" (Photo 2-8).

Blocks can also be used to showcase photographs. Four Shoo-fly blocks pieced with photo centers are grouped on the back of "Capezio Shoe-fly" (Photo 8-4).

If you want to get more adventuresome, try a pieced back. A simple one can be made from leftover fabrics from the front. The back of "Gaijin" (Photo 8-25) is an example.

Sometimes the back almost becomes a quilt top by itself. The back of "Make-believe Summer: At the Beach" (Photo 2-3) was made from leftover bits and pieces which didn't make the final selection for the front. The story of "Quake of '89" continues from the quilt front to the back (Photo 5-3). Since "Coming to Terms" has two themes, the Vietnam War and the Peace Movement, the

back is particularly significant. I really consider the back as the "other" front side (Photo 7-3).

Generally speaking, quilt backs are simpler and take less time and work than quilt fronts. They are visually designed and constructed in a shorter period of time. A pieced back does make the quilt a little less fun to quilt because of the additional seams. Keep this in mind as you are creating. For example, if there are two long seams near each other, adjust the location of the one on the back so it won't be in the way of the one on the front; it's impossible to line them up exactly. Don't worry about where the quilting pattern falls on the back. The design on the front takes precedence.

A rod pocket is a necessary part of a quilt that is to be hung. Notice how the rod pocket on the back of "Coming to Terms" has been pieced to match what is happening in the design lines of the back so it will be less noticeable (Photo 7-3).

QUILTING

Quilting stitches hold the quilt together. However, they can be more than a functional addition. Quilting can enhance the overall design and impact of the piece. I consider good quilting a gift to the viewer. Some quilters literally draw with their thread.

I usually make up my quilting designs as I go along. While I'm quilting one section, the design for another part will come to me. Since I personally have an aversion to marking my quilt tops, I only use free-form or straight lines that can be marked with tape and/or pins. Within these limitations, it's amazing the variety of designs still open to me.

If you don't want your quilting to show, use thread to blend with the area being quilted. If you want to show off your stitches and the patterns they form, use contrasting colors. As far as I'm concerned, it's perfectly acceptable to use more than one color of thread in quilting a piece, and I never worry about where colors end up on a decorative back.

Quilting Designs

Quilting can be used to enhance your story once you go beyond the basic outlining of shapes and pieces. Keep in mind a few simple things about quilted lines. Straight lines are stagnant. They can be organized in ordered patterns such as grids and used as filler in background areas. They can also be drawn randomly for a more contemporary look. Curved lines add movement. Excessive curved lines in an area add a feeling of confusion. Zigzag lines act in a similar way and can contribute frenzy.

Quilting designs don't have to be complex to be effective. Notice the quilted triangles in the sky in "Westward Ho!" (Photo 3-4). They contrast with the curved lines of the clouds which have been outline quilted. As I moved across the sky from right to left, time got shorter and shorter so I made my triangles bigger and bigger. The size change worked because the cactus on the left side is larger than the two on the right. Talk about luck! The end effect of the quilting just adds to the surreal Georgia O'Keeffe sky.

The quilting line can be an opportunity to reinforce the quilt theme. Notice the two designs I used to quilt the cactus itself (Photo 3-4). The zigzags are appropriate to the surface contours of the cactus. In another detail of the quilt (Photo 8-3), I used wave quilting to mirror the shape of my photo niche.

Let the fabric and theme speak to you as you design. For example, undulating lines are a common way to represent air and water flow. I used undulating lines in the ocean in "Make-believe Summer: At the Beach" (Photo 2-2) and in the background negative space in "Hanky for the Teacher" (Photo 4-3). Donna Holt designed dust swirls to be quilted into her quilt "Exodus: April 1942" (Photo 7-5).

Quilting designs don't have to be elaborate to be effective. Bonnie Holmstrand drafted a simple curve to use in "Minor Inconveniences." The central panel of her quilt was made from a combination of Bow Tie and Pinwheel blocks (Figure 8-26). Figure 8-27 shows the sketch page for her quilting design and how she drafted her simple "wave" curve to suggest the water of Prince William Sound.

Remember, quilting doesn't always have to be a design—it can also be an image. Bonnie Holmstrand added quilted scissors to "One Arm Bandit" (Photo 3-12). Jeanie Smith selected the graphic symbol of the flagger for "Lucy Flagbody Goes Fishing." She created an interlocking design of flaggers and directional arrows (Photo 8-26).

Hand and Machine Quilting

I love to hand quilt, but it is not a fast process—200 hours of stitching on a large quilt top is quite a chunk of time for most busy people, so be sure you enjoy the process before you commit yourself to it. With story quilts, however, the time spent can be very special as it provides additional "thinking" time about your subject.

If your time for quilting activities is limited or you don't particularly enjoy hand quilting, consider machine quilting some of your pieces. It takes some practice, but can look quite nice.

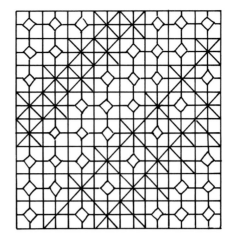

Figure 8-26. Sketch: *Minor Inconveniences.* Bonnie Bucknam Holmstrand.

Figure 8-27. Sketch: quilting design for *Minor Inconveniences.* Bonnie Bucknam Holmstrand.

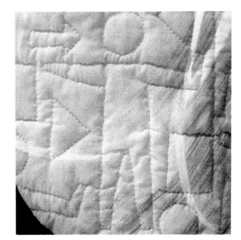

Photo 8-26. *Lucy Flagbody Goes Fishing* (detail: quilted flaggers and arrows). Jeanie Smith.

If you haven't machine quilted, read Harriet Hargrave's *Heirloom Machine Quilting*. It's necessary to think a little differently when you select your designs because the quilt is usually rolled and fed through the machine with only a long rectangular section being exposed at once. (Of course, this is much as you would view only a portion of the quilt on many quilting frames. However, in hand quilting, it's easy to unthread your needle when you've gone as far as you can in a direction and just leave the thread to take up later when the quilt has been rolled some more.)

Ideally, in machine quilting you want to keep going as far as possible in one sweep down the quilt without having to end your stitching line. Take as an example the design Bonnie Holmstrand selected for "Minor Inconveniences" (Figure 8-27). It would work well in machine quilting if you diagonally stitched the curves in a back-and-forth, zigzag pattern vertically down a row of blocks. If the same design were hand quilted, it could be worked in a long continuous line diagonally across the quilt, threading and unthreading the hand quilting needle as you went.

George Taylor machine quilted "Little Redheaded Girl." To enhance the ringlet theme, he used twin needles to stitch flowing lines over the background blocks. This was a very effective treatment and many viewers ask him how he did the trapunto (Photo 2-6).

You can also do both hand and machine quilting on the same quilt. The quilt can be sectioned off and the layers held together with utilitarian, basic stitching-in-the-ditch machine quilting with monofilament nylon. Then more noticeable decorative hand quilting can be added to areas where it will be showcased. Anne Ito did this when she quilted "Letting Go" (Photo 7-7). Since the quilt was such an emotional piece for her, she felt it was really important to spend time hand quilting it. Anne enjoyed the process so much she ended up adding much more hand quilting than she had originally intended.

A word of warning about mixing hand and machine quilting. If you want to enter your work in a quilt show, make sure there's a category for machine quilted items. Often the machine quilted category allows some hand quilting, but hand quilted categories always have 100% hand quilting as a requirement.

Sometimes you may find it impossible to quilt your quilt as heavily as you would really like to and still get the quilt done to meet a deadline. I have learned to devise quilting designs that can be elaborated on later, rather than committing myself to denser quilting from the beginning. In this way I can add layers of quilting to the piece, but show it between the light quilting and heavier quilting

stages. Since I use a portable Q Snap™ frame, I can bind the quilt and not worry about having to re-attach it to a stationary frame.

"Coming to Terms" (Photo 7-2) was quilted in this manner. Figure 8-28 shows the light quilting design I began with for the inside squares and the later added stitches. Figure 8-29 shows the beginning quilting pattern in the red connecting strips. It also shows the possibilities I came up with for additional quilting: I chose variation A.

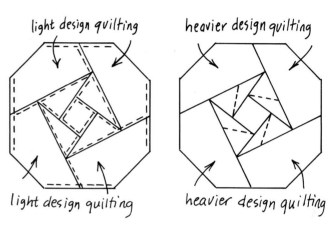

Sketch A: light quilting.   Sketch B: added quilting.

Figure 8-28. Quilting designs for *Coming to Terms* inner blocks. Mary Mashuta.

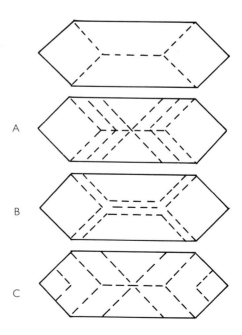

Figure 8-29. Sketches A, B, C: possible quilting designs for *Coming to Terms* grid. Mary Mashuta.

9. Techniques

Although *Story Quilts: Telling Your Tale in Fabric* can be read, enjoyed, and used by quilters of varying skill levels, it is not meant to be a basic text. My emphasis has been on stories and their translation to fabric. Color usage and design, in the context of story quilts, have also been emphasized. Countless other authors have done a good job of imparting basic techniques in their books and articles. I encourage you to read these texts for techniques not covered here.

I will, however, describe how to do raw-edge appliqué since it's a little unusual. First, though, let's consider the drafting and sewing of individual pieced blocks since this seems to be what is holding many quilters back from creating their own quilts. You will find this particularly helpful if you have concentrated on classes and books that have emphasized quick methods. Read the basic methods described here and then see if you can incorporate information and techniques you already know in creating new-to-you blocks.

MAKING BLOCKS

I am always amazed how many quilters haven't learned to draft their own quilt blocks and must limit themselves to only those blocks for which they can find existing published patterns. A whole world can open up for you when you discover how simple many blocks are to draft.

Since patchwork originated well before written rules and how-to books, there's more than one classification system around. Many, but not all, blocks can be divided into a grid to make them easier to decipher. Try to find the smallest square unit which makes up the block. Using it as a measure, count off the number of times it can be repeated along the edge. This usually makes it possible to see the basic grid. For example, one of the oldest block categories is the nine-patch. (See Figures 9-1 and 9-2 for examples of nine-patch blocks used in this book.)

If the block isn't a nine-patch, then look at what's happening along one edge and see if the units can be divided into multiples of four or five. Using this system, I can usually place additional blocks into one of the categories shown in Figures 9-3 through 9-6. While not all blocks will fit into the basic grid categories, it's surprising how many

will. One other simple type of block is made by two intersecting diagonal lines (Figure 9-7). Once these basics are mastered, you will have blocks to keep you busy for a long time. Harder to decode blocks can be mastered later.

As you come across block names, don't always settle for the first variation you find. Take the time to look at all the different variations. Often they may look completely

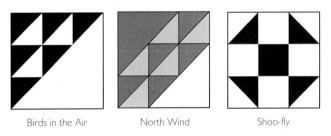

Birds in the Air North Wind Shoo-fly

Figure 9-1. Nine-patch. Two vertical and two horizontal lines intersect and divide the block into nine segments that make up the basic grid.

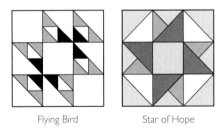

Flying Bird Star of Hope

Figure 9-2. Extended nine-patch. The individual units of the nine-patch grid can be subdivided with additional vertical and horizontal lines to form thirty-six segments. This is not called six-patch, however.

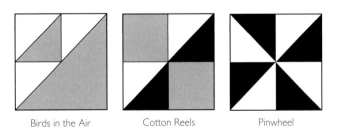

Birds in the Air Cotton Reels Pinwheel

Figure 9-3. Four-patch. One vertical and one horizontal line divide the grid into four segments. Some prefer to call this a two-patch.

81

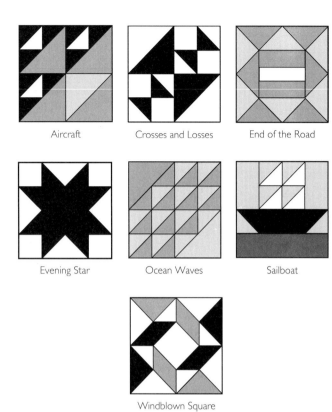

Aircraft Crosses and Losses End of the Road

Evening Star Ocean Waves Sailboat

Windblown Square

Figure 9-4. Extended four-patch. Three vertical and three horizontal lines divide the grid into sixteen segments.

Wind at Sea

Figure 9-5. Further extended four-patch. The grid is divided into 64 segments.

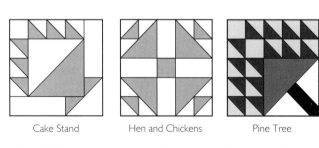

Cake Stand Hen and Chickens Pine Tree

Figure 9-6. Five-patch. Four vertical and four horizontal lines divide the grid into twenty-five segments.

different from each other. Some may be much more appealing than others. Part of a particular block's appeal can be that it is much simpler to piece, which may be important when you consider your skill level and time available.

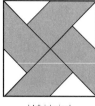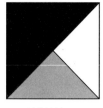

Figure 9-7. Intersecting diagonal. Two intersecting diagonal lines divide the block.

Whirlwind Wild Waves

DRAFTING

When you find blocks you like and feel you will be able to piece, it's time to draft them accurately. Determine what size you will need to make your blocks. Sometimes it's necessary to draw the block several sizes so you can decide which would work best.

Draw your basic grid on graph paper (4 or 8 squares to the inch). Draw in the individual divisions, shading them if that's helpful. To simplify your work, make individual pieces as big as possible. For example, if three adjoining triangles in your grid end up forming a larger triangle and are to be cut from the same fabric, then just draw one large triangle. The blocks Crosses and Losses and Hen and Chickens are examples of this. Sometimes adjoining segments can be joined to form new shapes which are still possible to piece easily. Windblown Square and Whirlwind are examples.

Next, look at your block and see how many pattern pieces you will need to draw. For example, the nine-patch blocks Birds in the Air, North Wind, and Shoo-fly need only two templates each.

Never cut up your drafted block to make templates. The drawing is sacred (like the puzzle box lid!) and should always be saved in case you need to refer to it later. If you wish, draw the seam allowances for the individual pieces right on the drawing of your block if you can keep from getting confused when there are multiple seam allowances to add. It's also okay to redraw the individual shapes elsewhere and then add a seam allowance to each. (If you do this, make sure to place the templates over the original drawing to check for accuracy after they're made.)

For the kind of blocks I like to draw, the supplies are simple: good quality graph paper, a mechanical or sharp number two pencil, and an eraser. I always use a C-Thru® ruler for my drafting. I like both the 18" and smaller 6" versions. It isn't difficult to add ¼" seam allowances to straight edges. Mistakes are more likely to occur when the seam allowance is added to a diagonal (Figure 9-8).

TEMPLATES

When the seam allowances have been added, place the template plastic over each shape and trace the outside

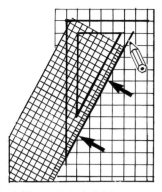 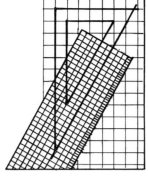

A. Move ruler back slightly to allow for pencil lead width. Draw.

B. Check accuracy by lining up two lines in the middle of the ruler.

Figure 9-8. Adding ¼" seam allowance to a diagonal line.

edge accurately onto the plastic. Several small pieces of tape will help hold the plastic in place. Cut out the shape, using scissors, rotary cutter, or X-Acto® knife.

If the pieces are oddly shaped, you may want to transfer the corner point to the template. I mark with a pencil and later punch a hole with an awl. A quarter-punch, which is a small paper punch, may also be used.

After the pieces have been cut out in plastic, hold them over the "originals" for an accuracy check. To make accurate patchwork, it is necessary to check yourself at each step as you go along.

ASSEMBLY

Arrange the block pieces near your sewing machine. (If they need to be removed from the pinup wall, arrange them on a tray or lightweight board so they stay in the proper order.) Here are a few simple rules to make assembly easier:

1. Most blocks can be divided into rows.
2. First join any smaller pieces that will form larger units.
3. Next join the individual units in a row to form a strip.
4. When the strips are complete, they can be joined to form the completed block.

As an example, let's devise a sewing system for the simple nine-patch Shoo-fly. A schematic drawing is shown in Figure 9-9.

1. Arrange the pieces in three rows.
2. Begin by picking up and sewing the four sets of triangles that need to be sewn together.

3. Reposition the sewn patches to make sure the triangles are turned the proper way.
4. Sew the three patches together in row one. Then sew the three patches together in row two and then those in row three.
5. Sew the completed row one to row two. Then add row three.

While many blocks may have more pieces than Shoo-fly, they are just as straightforward to assemble. More advanced blocks may take a little more time to figure out.

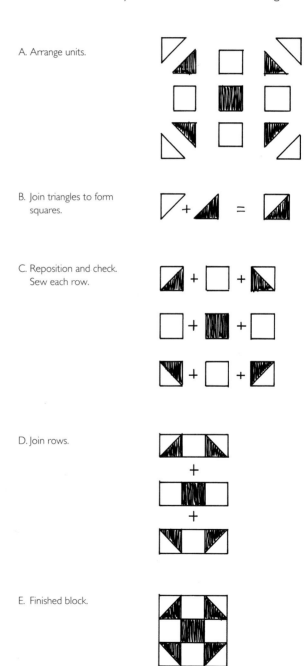

A. Arrange units.

B. Join triangles to form squares.

C. Reposition and check. Sew each row.

D. Join rows.

E. Finished block.

Figure 9-9. Schematic drawing: sewing Shoo-fly.

RAW-EDGE APPLIQUÉ BLOCKS

I had fun creating raw-edge appliqué blocks for "Make-believe Summer: Under the Umbrella" with its curved soft edges and "Westward Ho!" with its geometric edges. Both were machine stitched. The technique is a fast, immediate way to construct blocks. They may be either hand or machine quilted after they are joined together. Both sets of blocks were finished 6" × 6" blocks. To begin, I rotary-cut strips of fabric 6½" wide (to allow for seam allowances).

To create a soft-edge block as shown in Figure 9-10, do the following:

1. Use Fabric A for the background.
2. Cut Fabric B in a soft, freeflowing line across one end.
3. Place Fabric B on Fabric A and stitch ¼" from the flowing line. Trim away excess on the underneath side, making sure a ¼" seam allowance remains.
4. Repeat Steps 2 and 3 until a 6" block has been created.

To create a geometric block as shown in Figure 9-11, follow the same procedure as for making a soft-edge block, except make one change. In Step 2, fold the fabric strip in sections before you begin cutting. The more folds, the more jags you will get. (For finished results, see Photo 3-6.) It's also possible to use a straight line. However, this will ravel more since the long threads will still be intact.

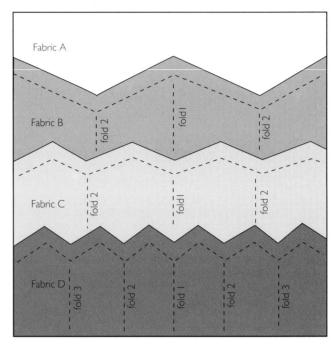

Figure 9-11. Creating a geometric raw-edge appliqué block.

SEWING TIPS

I only machine piece. All the quilts in this book that were pieced, were machine pieced. Not all machines are equally easy to use for machine piecing. If you are having trouble stitching, consider these solutions:

1. Replace the large hole throat plate used for zigzag stitching with a single-stitch throat plate. The hole will be smaller so it won't grab your fabric. (Danger: Do not try to stitch zigzag or move the needle position because the needle will break.)
2. Use a size 12 needle rather than a larger needle. It's a good size for most patchwork-weight fabric.
3. Use good needles and change them frequently. Dull needles snag fabrics.
4. Use only 100% cotton thread. Polyester thread builds up static electricity in your tension mechanism. Skipped stitches result.
5. I find 100% cotton fabrics are usually the easiest to stitch. If you're joining a cotton to a stretchy poly blend, put the blend on the bottom as you send it through the machine. A little spray starch can be used to stabilize stretchy fabrics.
6. Bias seams are easy to stretch as they are sewn. If at all possible, join a bias-cut edge to a straight-cut edge. Place the bias-cut edge on the bottom next to the feed dogs so they can work in any extra fullness.

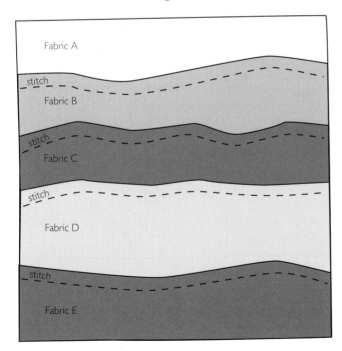

Figure 9-10. Creating a soft raw-edge appliqué block.

Contrary to popular belief, most machine presser feet are not ¼" wide. If you are having trouble stitching accurate ¼" seams, try the following:

1. Move the needle position. (My Bernina can be moved one step to the right. The resulting seam is a scant ¼".)
2. Add a long piece of tape to your machine exactly ¼" from the needle. (This works best on a straight stitching machine like the Singer® Featherweight portable. If your machines zigzags, the feed dogs are wider and you may only be able to run the tape up to them.)
3. Purchase a Little Foot™ presser foot which has a true ¼" edge. At first, using it may seem awkward, but with practice, the results are wonderful. As you practice, check your sewn seam with a grided ruler to insure accuracy. (It is available for most machines, including the Singer slant needle. Some machines, like the Bernina, require an adapter. Consult the list of sources in the Appendix.)

Here are some pinning tips:

1. Use long slender sharp pins. Ilse pins or the long ones with glass heads are examples. They give you more to hold onto with the tips of your fingers if you need to stabilize the piece during stitching.
2. Place the pins with the heads away from the edge, the opposite of the way you were taught in dressmaking. Since the seam allowance is narrow, this eliminates the possibility of driving over the heads when you stitch.
3. When pinning two pieces of patchwork together, always pin the two ends first. Then place a pin in the middle. More pins can be added, if necessary, after these three are in place. Remember, if there is any fullness, divide it evenly and place the side with the fullness *next* to the feed dogs.

4. Leave pins in while you are sewing patchwork. They help to stabilize the piece. I press down on them with my fingers if I'm having trouble sending the piece through the presser foot and feed dogs in a straight path.

PRESSING TIPS

Good pressing techniques are an integral part of sewing. They are just as important in patchwork as they are in garment construction. Buy yourself a good iron and use it often. Make sure it has plenty of steam holes and a "shot of steam" feature. Here are a few pressing tips:

1. Create a small pressing center near your sewing machine, so it isn't necessary to get up all the time to press. (I use a Portapress—the address is in the Appendix.)
2. Press into a thick terry cloth towel so seam ridges won't be so apparent.
3. After two patchwork pieces have been joined with stitching, press them flat as they lay, before opening the piece up for further pressing. (If both stitched edges were bias, press both sides of the joined unit before opening.)
4. In general, don't press seams open. Instead, press both in the same direction. If possible, press dark fabrics toward the dark side rather than the light so they won't shadow through.
5. Press a seam before it is crossed with another seam.
6. Give quilt tops a good touch-up press before basting them.
7. Carefully press quilts when you have finished quilting them. Watch your iron temperature. You don't want to melt a polyester batt!

Many quilters have never considered the last two steps, but I am often told how nice and flat my quilts are. I'm not into puff. I prefer the cotton-type batts. Pressing and batt selection give me the results I want.

Conclusion

Whether you are a novice or an experienced quilter, I hope you now have ample ideas so you can create your own personal story quilt. I hope you enjoyed the quilts and their stories as much as I have enjoyed collecting them.

When planning your own story quilt, be realistic about your skills and time commitment. Part of the planning process should entail designing a quilt that you can finish. Employ fast methods when they don't detract from the overall design, but when necessary, learn to enjoy the process of creating rather than "generating" a quilt. Remember, fast is not always best, only faster.

One last story before I leave you. When I was teaching in Alaska, I met Susie Silook, a Siberian Eskimo ivory carver. Even though carving is a task traditionally done by men, her brother had taught her to carve. When I told her I was a quilter, she said the women of her tribe said she was "without a thimble" because she didn't sew. This made me realize that just as Susie uses walrus ivory and her carving tools to tell her stories, I use my fabric, sewing machine, needle, thread, and "thimble" to tell my stories. And am I glad I have them.

Patterns

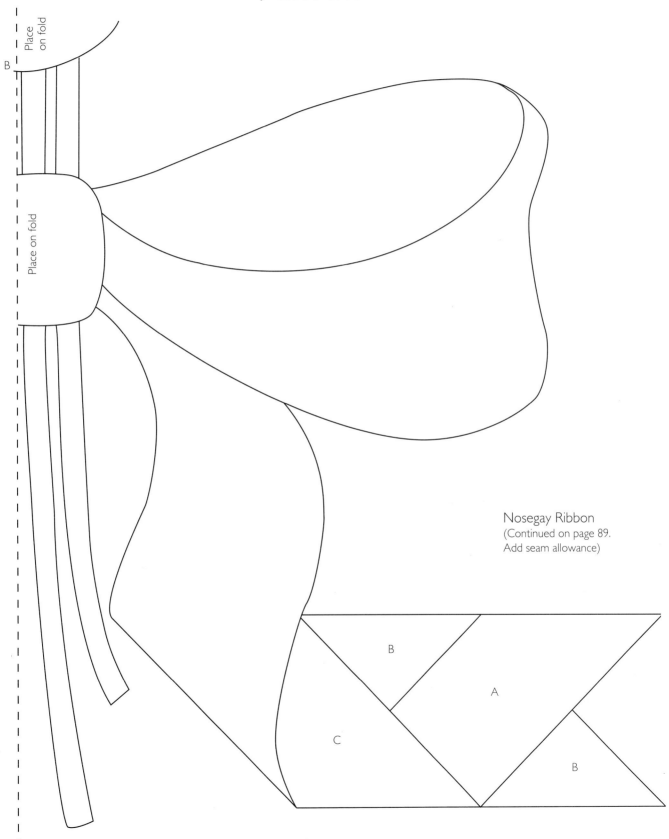

B

Place on fold

Place on fold

Nosegay Ribbon
(Continued on page 89.
Add seam allowance)

B

A

C

B

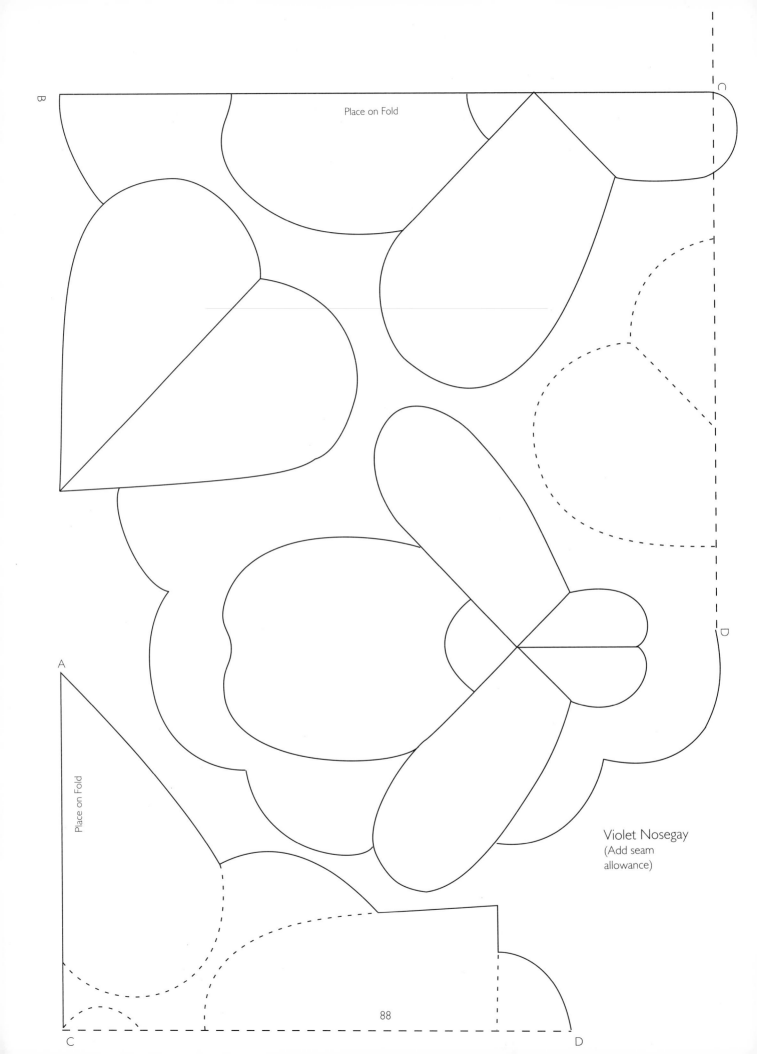

B

C

Place on Fold

A

Place on Fold

Violet Nosegay
(Add seam
allowance)

D

C

D

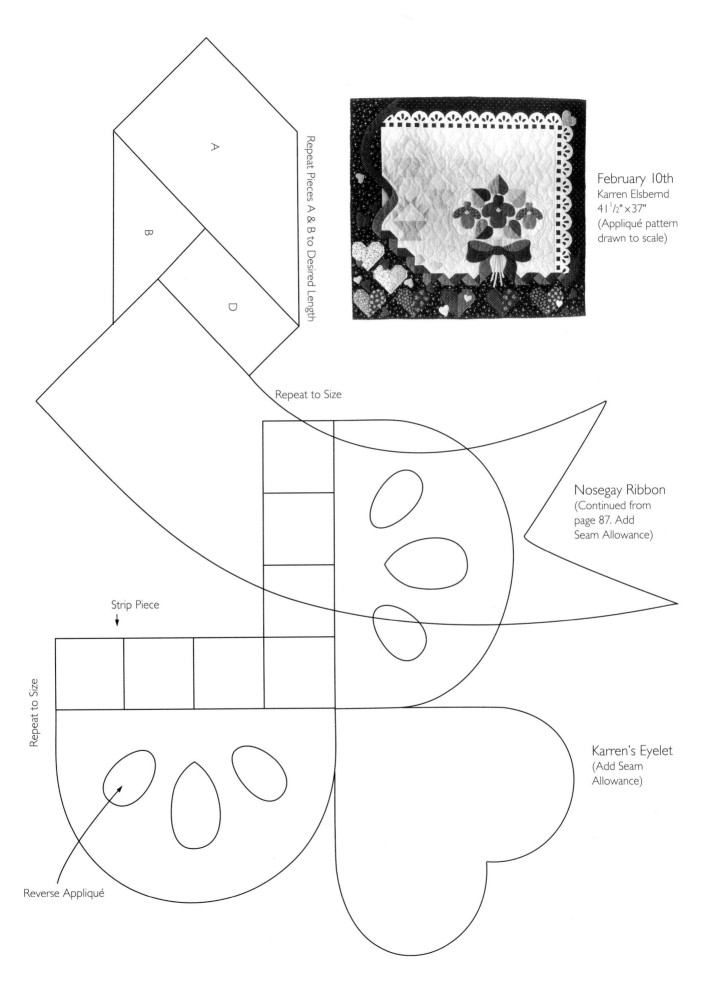

A

B

D

Repeat Pieces A & B to Desired Length

Repeat to Size

February 10th
Karren Elsbernd
41¹/₂" × 37"
(Appliqué pattern
drawn to scale)

Nosegay Ribbon
(Continued from
page 87. Add
Seam Allowance)

Strip Piece

Repeat to Size

Karren's Eyelet
(Add Seam
Allowance)

Reverse Appliqué

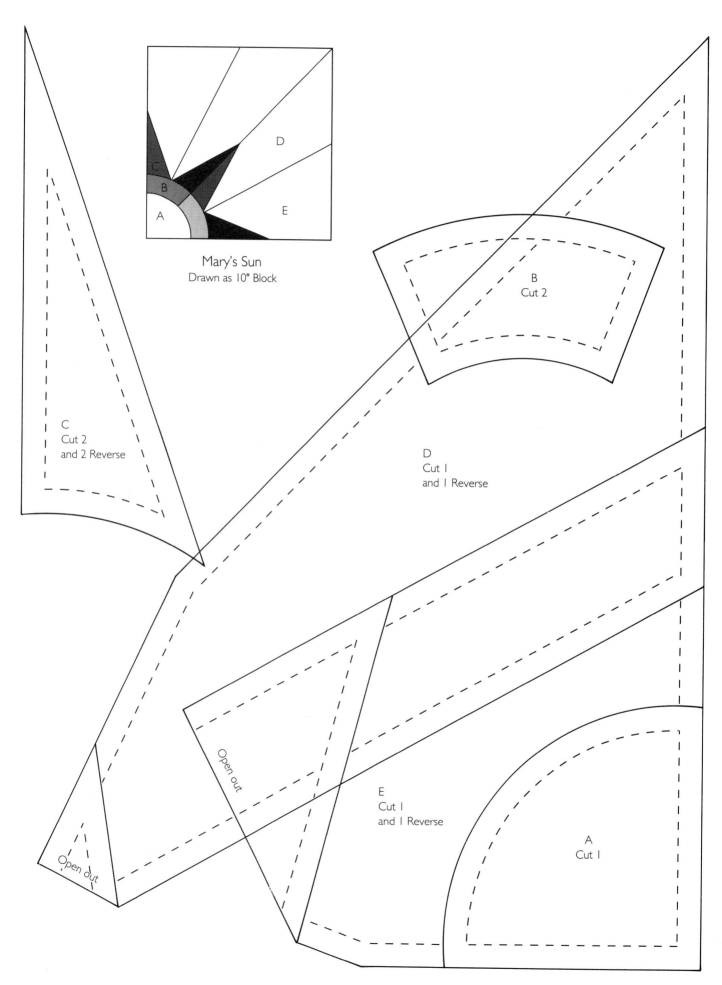

Mary's Sun
Drawn as 10" Block

B
Cut 2

C
Cut 2
and 2 Reverse

D
Cut 1
and 1 Reverse

Open out

Open out

E
Cut 1
and 1 Reverse

A
Cut 1

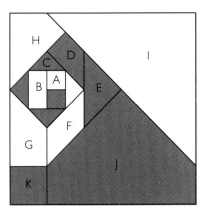

Mary's Ocean
Drawn as 10" Block

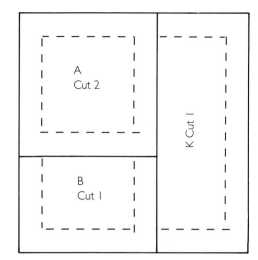

A
Cut 2

B
Cut 1

K Cut 1

D
Cut 1

H Cut 1

G
Cut 1

I Cut 1

J Cut 1

F
Cut 1

E Cut 1

C Cut 1

Place on Fold

Place on Fold

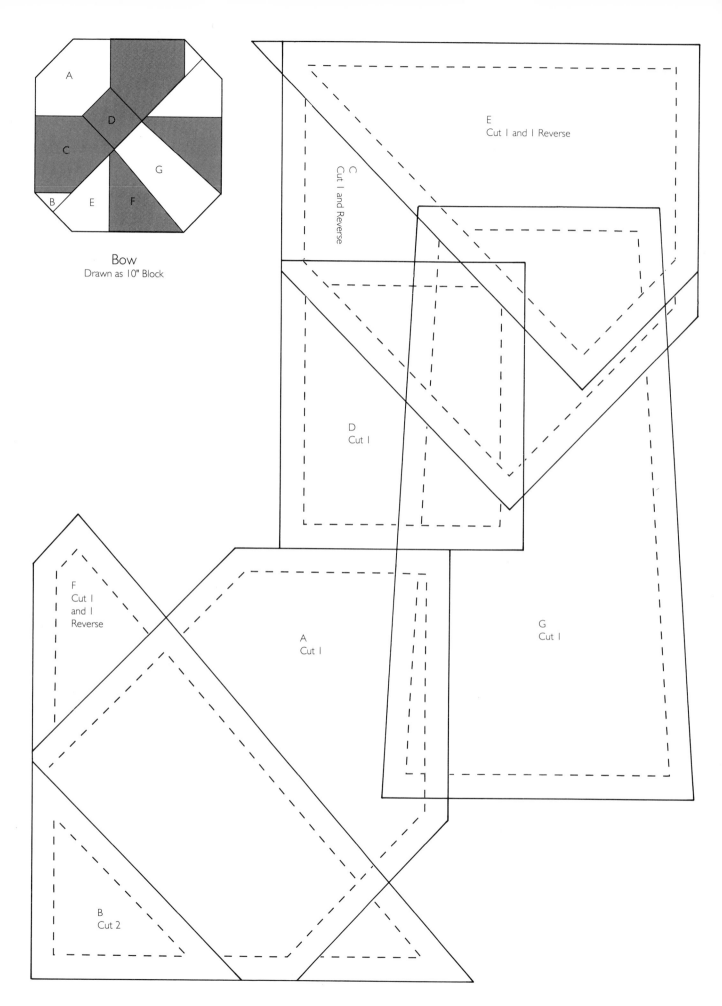

A

B

C
Cut 1 and Reverse

D
Cut 1

E
Cut 1 and 1 Reverse

F
Cut 1
and 1
Reverse

A
Cut 1

G
Cut 1

B
Cut 2

Bow
Drawn as 10" Block

Bibliography

Many of the books noted here have been self-published or are available from less well-known publishers; for those, I have included addresses. Contact the author/publisher directly if you are unable to locate a copy in your local quilt store or public library.

Beyer, Jinny. *Patchwork Patterns*. 1003 Turkey Run Road, McLean, VA 22101: EPM Publications, 1979.

Beyer, Jinny. *The Quilter's Album of Blocks and Borders*. 1003 Turkey Run Road, McLean, VA 22101: EPM Publications, 1980.

Brackman, Barbara. *Encyclopedia of Pieced Quilt Patterns*. 500 Louisiana Street, Lawrence, KS 66044: Prairie Flower Publishing, 1984.

Burns, Jan. "A Special Exhibition: Quilts from an Earthquake." *Creative Quilting*, Vol. 6, No. 3, May/June 1991.

Croner, Marjorie. *Fabric Photos*. 306 North Washington Avenue, Loveland, CO 80537: Interweave Press, 1989.

"Earthquake Quilts." *Patchwork Quilt* Tsūshin, No. 42, 1991.

"Gaijin: American Quilters Visit Japan." *Patchwork Quilt* Tsūshin, No. 22, 1988.

Hargrave, Harriet. *Heirloom Machine Quilting*. Lafayette, CA: C & T Publishing, 1990.

Hopkins, Judy. *Fit to Be Tied*. Bothell, WA: That Patchwork Place, 1989.

Khin, Yvonne M. *The Collector's Dictionary of Quilt Names*. Washington, DC: Acropolis Books, 1980 (1985 reprint).

Malone, Maggie. *1001 Patchwork Designs*. New York: Sterling Publishing, 1982.

Martin, Judy. *Judy Martin's Ultimate Book of Quilt Block Patterns*. 3030 Upham Court, Denver, CO 80215: Crosley-Griffith Publishing, 1988.

Martin, Judy. *Scraps, Blocks and Quilts*. 3030 Upham Court, Denver, CO 80215: Crosley-Griffith Publishing, 1990.

Mashuta, Mary. "Earthquake Quilts." *American Quilter*, Vol. 6, No. 3, Summer 1991.

———. "Gaijin: American Quilters Visit Japan." *American Quilter*, Vol. 4, No. 2, Summer 1988.

———. *Wearable Art for Real People*. Lafayette, CA: C & T Publishing, 1989.

Millard, Debra. *A Quilter's Guide to Fabric Dyeing*. 922 Madison, Denver, CO 80206: Debra Millard Lunn, 1984.

Pasquini, Katie. *3 Dimensional Design*. Lafayette, CA: C & T Publishing, 1988.

Rehmel, Judy. *The Quilt I.D. Book*. New York: Prentice-Hall, 1986.

Appendix – Sources

Alaska Dyeworks
Susan Roberts
300 West Swanson, Suite 101
Wasilla, AK 99687
907-373-6562
Hand-dyed cottons (progressions, batiks, mottles, crackles, and marbles)

Sonya Lee Barrington
837 47th Avenue
San Francisco, CA 94121
415-221-6510
Hand-dyed marbled and printed cottons

Blue-Printables
P.O. Box 1201
Burlingame, CA 94011-1201
800-356-0445
Special fabric for photo negative transfers

By Jupiter!
Pictures to Fabric
6033 North 17th Avenue
Phoenix, AZ 85015
602-242-2574
Transfer gel for pictures to fabric

The Cotton Patch
Carolie Hensley
1025 Brown Avenue
Lafayette, CA 94549
510-284-1177
Quilting fabric and supplies, including Ilse pins, etc.

Fabric Fotos
Charlene Bulls
3801 Olsen, #3
Amarillo, TX 79109
806-359-8241
Photos transferred to fabric

Little Foot, Ltd.
Lynn Graves
605 Bledsoe NW
Albuquerque, NM 87107
505-345-7647
Special sewing machine foot for ¼" stitching (standard short shank, Singer slant needle, and Pfaff 1200 Series; Bernina will need an adapter)

Lunn Fabrics
Debra Lunn
357 Santa Fe
Denver, CO 80223
303-377-1913
Hand-dyed cottons (solids and patterns)

M'ART Designs
Marit Lee Kacera
30 St. Albans Street South, #5
St. Paul, MN 55105
612-222-2483
Hand-dyed cottons and silks (solids and patterns)

Picture This
Fashion Show
Plaid Enterprises
1649 International Boulevard
Box 7600
Norcross, GA 30091-7600
404-923-8200
Transfer medium for photocopies to fabric

Portapress
Emily Tughan
Studio North, Inc.
P.O. Box 463
Manistee, MI 49660
Portable ironing board

Q Snap Frame
Lamb Art Press
P.O. Box 38
Parsons, TN 38363
901-847-7155
Portable, break-apart quilting frames

Seminole Sampler
Savage Mill
71 Mellor Avenue
Catonsville, MD 21228
410-788-1720
Solid cottons, quilting supplies

Shades, Inc.
Stacy Michell
2880 Holcomb Bridge Road, Suite B-9
Alpharetta, GA 30202
1-800-783-DYED
Hand-dyed cottons and silks (solids, special effects, and textures). Catalog $5.00

Stitchless Fabric Glue and Transfer Medium
Delta Technical Coatings, Inc.
Slomons Adhesives
2550 Pellissier Place
Whittier, CA 90601
818-579-5420
Transfer medium for photocopies to fabric

About the Author

Mary Mashuta's love of fabric and color began in childhood and led to two degrees in Home Economics. She has been an active member of the San Francisco Bay Area quilt community since the early 1970s. In 1985, she began to work full-time on her quilt-related interests, including designing, writing, and teaching. She has taught nationally and in Canada and South Africa.

Mary is the author of *Wearable Art for Real People* where she introduced her innovative color concept of pushed neutrals, the origami biscuit puff, using pieced stripes in garments, and the concepts of "body uniqueness" and "flamboyance quotient." She is a repeat Fairfield Processing Fashion Show participant, and her garments have won awards in the American Quilter's Society Annual Fashion Show.

Professional experience in the interior design field fostered an avid interest in quilt studios. Her informative articles on studios, wearables, and quilts have appeared in national publications, including *Quilter's Newsletter Magazine, American Quilter, Lady's Circle Patchwork Quilts,* and *Threads.* She has also been featured in Japanese, French, and South African magazines.

Mary enjoys creating story quilts detailing her experiences, and she loves to help others discover how to make their own quilts more personal. Her award-winning quilts have been shown internationally. As a professionaly trained teacher, Mary encourages confidence in quilters of varying skill levels.

Photo by Roberta Horton.